Perimeters,
Boundaries
and
Borders

The production of this catalogue was supported by Manchester Metropolitan University's Institute for Research and Innovation in Art and Design.

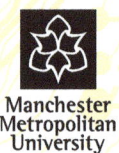 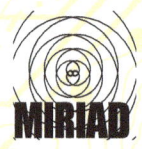

Editor and Designer: John Marshall
Sub Editor: Cezanne Charles
Publisher: Fast-uk

Fast-uk
c/o Manchester Metropolitan University
Department of Fine Arts
Grosvenor Building, Cavendish Street
Manchester M15 6BR
United Kingdom

www.fastuk.org.uk

ISBN 978-0-6152-1355-2

Table of Contents

Introduction

Fast-uk (Fine Art Science & Technology in the UK) is an artist-led organisation dedicated to promoting and encouraging practitioners that use digital and or electronic technologies as part of their practice. Based in Manchester, Fast-uk supports those working in this area through exhibition and networking opportunities. Fast-uk was established out of two concurrent activities the Higher Education Funding Council for England's 'Creating Art with Layer Manufacture Project' and the Department of Fine Arts at Manchester Metropolitan University hosting 'isea98terror' (International Symposium on Electronic Art).

I originally founded Fast-uk in 1997, to support sculptors working with 3D computer technologies. With the 'Perimeters, Boundaries, and Borders' (PBB) exhibition in 2006, Fast-uk evolved to support the creative application of technology by a broader selection of practitioners. For many of the disciplines within art and design the computer has taken its place alongside traditional means of working as an almost natural progression over the past decade. During this time we have witnessed a tremendous development in 3D computing applications and this has impacted on the ways in which many disciplines now conceive of and practice their activity.

The aim of this exhibition was to present the very latest examples of work that blur the conventional boundaries of art and design practice through the use of technology. The PBB activities included an exhibition (comprised of 4 new commissions and 16 selected works), a public symposium, and a free one day workshop on the use of the Open Source 3D application 'Blender' (led by Julian Oliver).

Fast-uk partnered with folly on the presentation of 'PBB' as part of the f.city Festival of Digital Culture. Without this partnership Fast-uk would have not been able to fully realise our plans. This was a great opportunity to expand our remit and reach a new audience. PBB was funded by Arts Council England, MIRIAD (Manchester Institute for Research and Innovation in Art and Design) and Lancaster City Council.

I would like to thank John Marshall and Cezanne Charles who worked tirelessly to ensure the success of this venture. Thanks are also due to Professor John Hyatt, Director of MIRIAD for his contribution to PBB and for the continued support given to Fast-uk over the years.

Keith Brown
Executive Director and Co-curator
www.fastuk.org.uk

As Founder and Executive Director of Fast-uk Keith Brown has done much to encourage and support digital art at a national and international level. A postgraduate student at the Royal College of Art 1972-75, for the past twenty years he has directed his research and practice from within the digital arena. His work embraces a wide range of digital media, including, 2D, 3D, 4D, time-based installation and video animation. Brown has recently exhibited in Japan, Australia, New Zealand, Turkey, the USA, Africa, France, Czech Republic, Poland, Germany, Austria and the UK. He has shown his work in venues such as the Royal Academy of Arts Summer Exhibition (London) 2002, 2003 & 2005, and the SIGGRAPH Art Gallery (San Diego, Los Angeles & Boston) 2003, 2004 & 2006. He is Professor of Sculpture and Digital Technologies at Manchester Metropolitan University.

Perimeters, Boundaries and Borders

Fast-uk has been developing exhibitions since 1999. Reflecting on these previous exhibitions we wanted to take Fast-uk in a new direction - one that explored computer-based technologies and hybrid art and design practices. The result was 'Perimeters, Boundaries and Borders'.

personal computers has transformed the means by which we communicate, carry out work and entertain ourselves. Until now, the discourse surrounding these developments has primarily focused on the benefits this has brought for productivity and has only very recently touched upon the possibilities for the way practitioners work. Architects, artists, craft-makers, designers, engineers, and others are now using a common digital toolset. Digital information can be used for multiple purposes and this can ultimately lead to the breakdown of boundaries between disciplines.

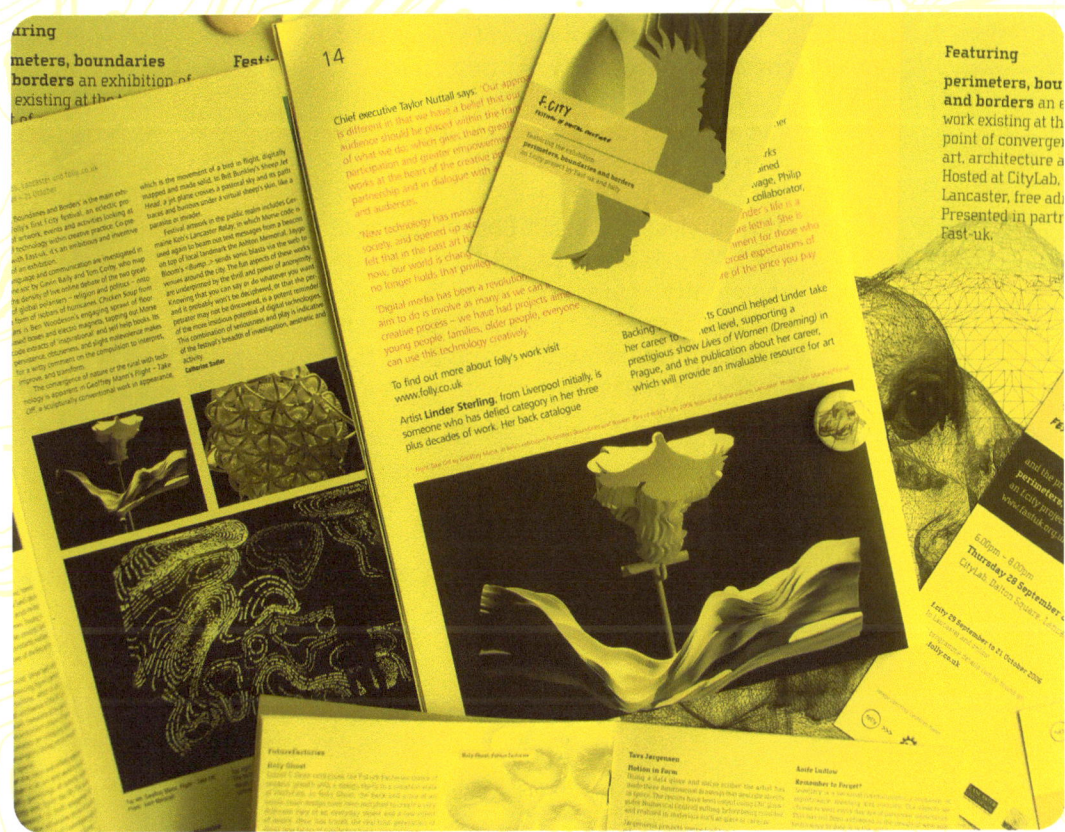

This title serves to indicate that this exhibition should be viewed as the sum of a set of 'in-betweens' - a negative space that grants permission to rethink the nature of creative practice driven by computer-based technologies. The exhibition does not try to define what should be inside or outside these edges - it attempts to present examples that can be viewed to cross-over or even ignore these kinds of distinctions.

Since the mid 1990s the growth in ownership of relatively powerful, cheap,

From this perspective the definitions that have traditionally separated artistic practice and design practice are in some cases becoming increasingly difficult to define. The binary point of view of either 'art' or 'design' seems over-simplified. It is contingent upon constructing in our minds a switch with 'art' at one pole and 'design' at the other. The works in this exhibition do not fit into this conception of the world. Rather, they are drawn from the plurality of composite forms to be found towards the middle of a sliding scale with purely aesthetic purposes at one end and purely utilitarian purposes at the other.

This is nothing new. From the time of the Renaissance onwards creative practitioners have worked across the areas that have come to be thought of as the fine and applied arts. This was brought to the forefront in the technological levelling-out of traditional, disciplinary distinctions that was a critical driver of De Stijl in the Netherlands, the Bauhaus in Germany and Russian Constructivism in the early 20th Century. The architects, artists and designers working in these historical movements saw industrial modes of production as a means of supporting the mass availability of products, the promotion of a machine-derived aesthetic and an opportunity to move art into everyday life.

Nevertheless, the practitioners featured in the 'PBB' exhibition do not form a unified community of practice. They do not share a singular goal or purpose. Rather they represent a community of interest - the clustering of a multitude of practices emerging at the current time.

These practitioners

- have made objects that exploit the unique capabilities of computer-based design and fabrication tools (e.g. Bunkley; Jørgensen; Mann; and Husslein)
- are investigating the processes involved in the conception, production and also the consumption of the objects and experiences they produce (e.g. Blackmore; Tabei & Miyauchi; and Ludlow)
- are engaging with new sets of technologically-driven, creative, cultural and economic conditions (e.g. FutureFactories; Marshall; NIO; and .MGX)
- and are looking beyond standard means of production to explore the deeper metaphysical dimensions of objects and experiences (e.g. Woodeson; Somlai-Fischer, Sjölén & Haque; Baily & Corby and Human Beans)

The co-curators anticipated that through this exhibition (and the complementary

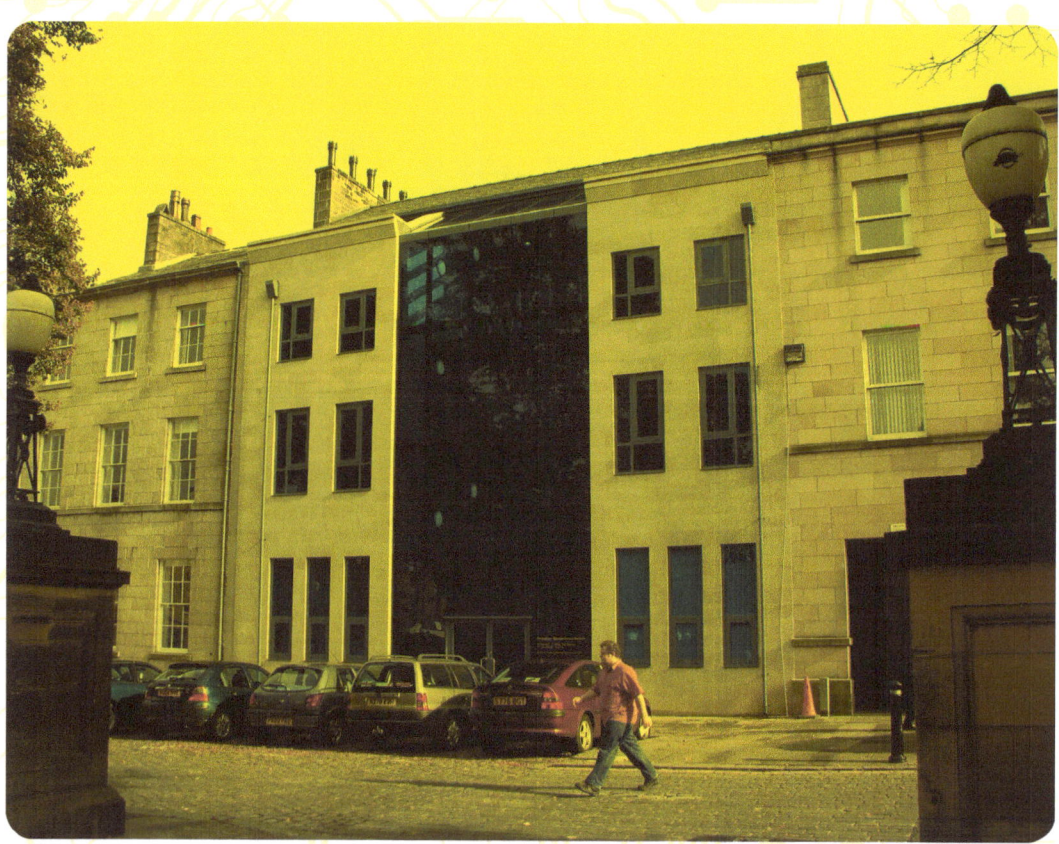

symposium) that practitioners and audiences alike would be able to make new connections between works that on the surface are apparently unrelated. CityLab - the building used for the exhibition - was a recently-renovated business centre for the creative industries in Lancaster (see p. 15). The ground floor offices and circulation spaces were used for the exhibition - making a link between cultural products and spaces earmarked for future cultural production. We hoped that this would lead to the exhibition being read as a series of possibilities - a means of exploring designed objects in-between the white cube of the traditional gallery space and the fluorescent glare of a strictly commercial context.

At the end of the Wachowski brothers' 1999 film 'The Matrix' Keanu Reeves' character 'Neo' calls up the machine world that controls an enslaved humanity and declares:

"...I'm going to show these people what you don't want them to see. I'm going to show them a world without you, a world without rules and controls, without borders or boundaries, a world where anything is possible. Where we go from there, is a choice I leave to you."

The aim of the 'PBB' exhibition was to point at a hybrid cultural discourse that can be seen to emerge in the space between conventional art and design disciplines through the use of common technologies. The exhibition doesn't represent a world without 'rules and controls' per se - just one that is perhaps less rigid in its adherence to the conventional borders and boundaries of art and design practice as they have previously been known.

Dr. John Marshall
Artistic Director and Curator
www.fastuk.org.uk

As an artist, designer and curator John Marshall has undertaken collaborations with architects, landscape designers, theatre companies, engineers and other artists. Marshall has presented and published his research in China, Denmark, the Netherlands, the UK and the US. Since 1998, Marshall has worked within rootoftwo (a collaborative partnership with Cezanne Charles) undertaking both self-initiated and commissioned projects in art and design. In addition to his work with Fast-uk, Marshall also curates exhibitions and urban screenings with other artist-led groups such as Video In the Built Environment (v1b3) and artcore and he is a member of the Upgrade! International network. He is an Assistant Professor at University of Michigan's School of Art and Design and was recently awarded a PhD from Robert Gordon University for his work exploring hybrid art and design practice using computer-based design and fabrication tools.

Design Now

Design now, perhaps necessarily, transcends many traditional subject areas. Designers no longer reside comfortably in categories such as product, furniture and graphics. Tony Dunne, Head of Interaction Design at the Royal College of Art, London states: "New hybrids of design are emerging. People don't fit in neat categories; they're a mixture of artists, engineers, designers, thinkers. They're in that fuzzy space and might be finding it quite tough, but the results are really exciting." (West, 2007).

I don't think this is a grand revelation. Design has always been viewed as a bridge between technology and art (Flusser, 1999). However, I think what is new is that designers and design companies in general are now faced with adopting and utilising techniques and approaches that

categorise or distinguish the changes that design faces at the moment. In my view these changes are threefold:

• Professional - a blurring of traditional design disciplines
• Economical - the transformation of funding and employment patterns
• Technological - developments in computing and manufacturing power

In an article in Design Week (Seymour, 2006), Richard Seymour (who is a partner in Seymour Powell - a relatively well-known design consultancy in London) is on record stating that design is mutating. He actually claims that design is on the verge of splitting into two separate disciplines. He states that what is needed in a modern, dynamic and highly competitive world is a different breed of designer – the "hybrid" perhaps? Seymour suggests there are two types of designer. One he terms the "specialist executor" and the

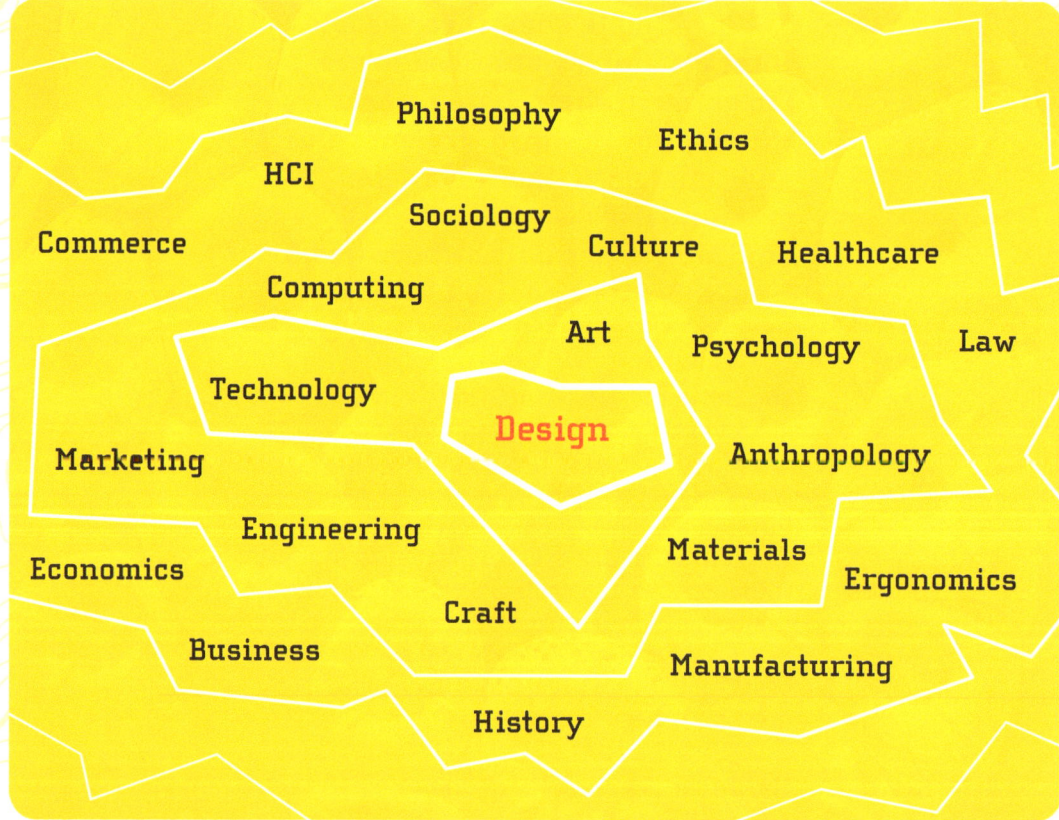

until recently have been comparatively uncommon to them. So we can say that designers are now asked to transcend many distinct disciplines. I've tried to

second is the "polymath interpolator" and he says that sometimes you come across both – an individual who has both qualities but these are very, very rare.

This interdisciplinary working practice is exemplified by Human Beans in the way that they merge commercial culture and design and disseminate it via non conventional routes such as spam, ambient media, shop shelves and exhibitions. Their "What's Cooking Grandma?" installation in the 'PBB' exhibition illustrates the range of disciplines that they frequently blend – design, advertising, and film.

In terms of economic and funding change there has been a lot of debate on the electronic forums recently such as ID Forum[1] and the DRS Forum[2] about the number of design graduates that we are actually producing in this country in particular and throughout the world in general. Obviously, this is partly the result of the huge pressures being exerted at a national, regional and local level. The range of postgraduate qualifications available today in the UK extend to: DPhil, MA, MA Res, MCA, M Des, MAD, M Ent, MFA, MG Prac, MH Prac, M Lit, MM Prac, MPhil, PhD, M Res, MSc, MSc Res, MST, BDC, PDD – the list goes on and on. I don't know how many there are - maybe around twenty different postgraduate qualifications and I think that there are at a rough estimate about a thousand postgraduate courses on offer in the UK. Probably more than half of them are in a design-related field. So I think there are massive pressures and change ahead in terms of economics and funds available.

The most obvious change is the blending of computing technologies in and across creative disciplines that has enabled designers to transcend what we've historically seen as distinct and separate design disciplines. I think we can observe many similarities today between the working practices of what we would once have distinguished as fine art and what we distinguish as design. Alex Coles has made use of the term "DesignArt" in his study of the blurring between art and design (Coles, 2005; Coles, 2007). I would imagine that most of us, if not all of us would recognise the work of Grayson Perry (Jones, 2007) who won the Turner Prize a few years ago. What is interesting about Grayson Perry's work is that his objects sell

[1] www.lsoft.com/scripts/ wl.exe?SL1=IDFORUM&H=Y ORKU.CA

[2] www. designresearchsociety.org

for thousands of pounds, they are generally found in prestigious galleries across the world and in terms of batch size we are talking small - we are talking mainly one offs but maybe limited editions of between one, five, ten. Then, if we look at the work of the acclaimed Dutch designer Hella Jongerius (Schouwenberg, 2003) then there are some very striking similarities between them. Jongerius' ceramic work, like Perry's pots, also sells for thousands of pounds and is commonly found in art galleries throughout the world and similarly the batch is very small – sometimes one offs, sometimes a range of five or ten. I think what is interesting about Hella Jongerius is that you can now trot along to IKEA and get your very own Hella Jongerius vase for a lot less money.

But where does art finish and design begin? We are in an era where designers and architects such as Ron Arad, the Campana Brothers, Gaetano Pesce and Frank Gehry choose to exhibit their work at Art Basel Miami Beach and where design products such as Zaha Hadid's prototype "Aqua" table sells at a New York City auction for almost $300,000. It is somewhat ironic that by returning to yesteryear's tradition of artisanship and patronage that designers are finally striking it rich. With the rise of the collectables market, designers can now make more money selling one or two pieces than they can from royalties. Nowadays artists and designers are almost indistinguishable in their respective working practices. According to the critically acclaimed designer Jaime Hayon: "Design is not really design anymore. For a long time art has been questioning what is art? Now we're asking what is design, and the funny thing is that design sometimes looks more like art than art does." (Hayon, 2007). In the context of 'PBB', the work of Lionel T. Dean bridges neatly the fine line between art and design. Dean is interested in the mass individualisation of products using rapid prototyping technologies and although trained as a designer his current work with FutureFactories takes something of a fine art approach in the production of his "personally produced" chairs.

The next comparison expands on the fine

line that I am trying to indicate which exists between what we routinely see as artists and designers. If we explore the work of Martí Guixé (Guixé, 2002) a fairly well known Catalan designer (who actually refers to himself as an ex-designer) and the work of the artist David Shrigley (Paul, 2003) then we can see that there are very many more similarities in their work and their working processes than there are differences. What is extremely noticeable is that they both have a very similar look and feel in their creative output. The often respective, clumsy, full cap, hand-written scribbles they both employ is very

[3] www.thwartdesign.com

of economic or funding change – its pretty boring really – let's not get too depressed about it. But in terms of how technology has altered design I think that is fairly obvious. Technology has certainly altered design in the context of Karim Rashid - and perhaps for the worse. Rashid has relentlessly produced blob after blob and he has attracted heavy criticism and I think some of it is justified. But there appears no end to the long list of clients that queue up for his services. I think he's tried to coin a new aesthetic - blobjects or blobism or blobitecture or superblob or something. Thwart Design[3] are one of the

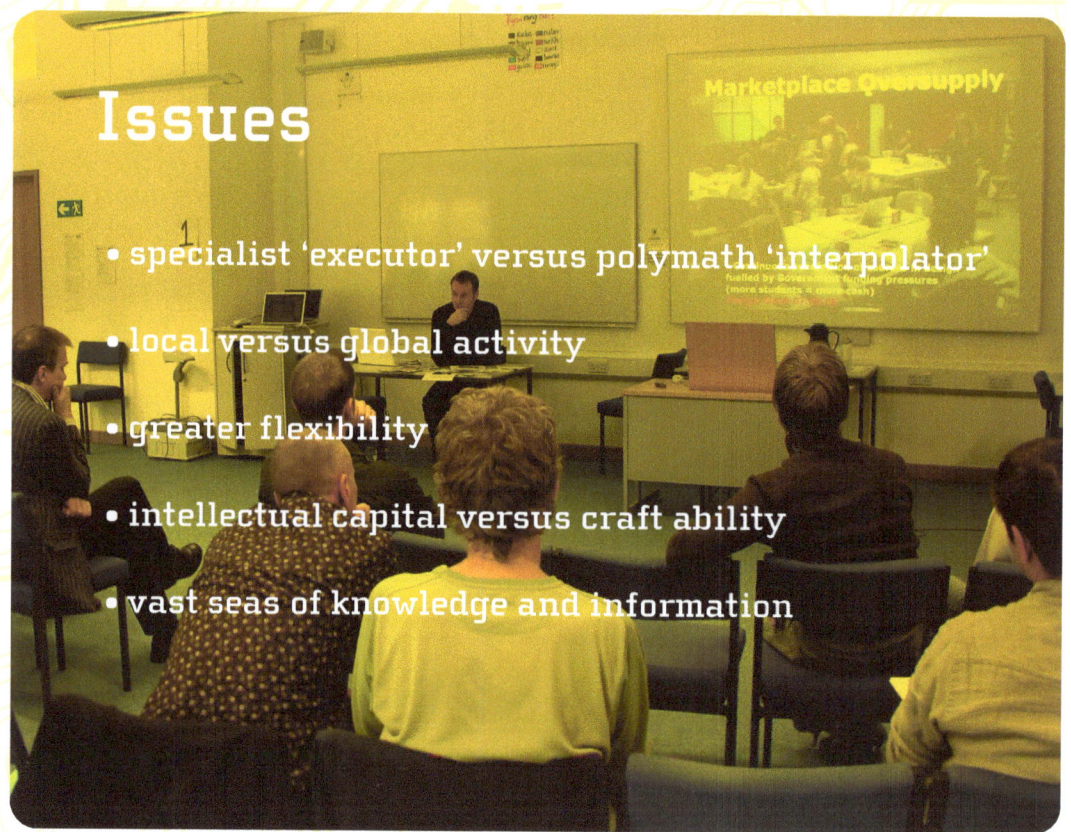

Issues

- specialist 'executor' versus polymath 'interpolator'
- local versus global activity
- greater flexibility
- intellectual capital versus craft ability
- vast seas of knowledge and information

close. Similarly, if we look at their work – a lot of Marti Guixé's work is based in the dematerialisation of products – he funds a lot of these exploratory works by his day job which is the interior designer of every Camper shop throughout the world. Again there are similarities to his work and Shrigley's and some of those similarities include the way that both of them treat subjects such as tattoos and also their use of everyday objects in new contexts.

I don't really have any examples to show

groups who have criticised this aesthetic shift towards the "blobular" style. They pronounce that we must "break the blob... and design with an edge". Certainly we can describe the work of Tavs Jørgensen, from the 'PBB' exhibition, as having a technological edge. Like Rashid and others, Jørgensen straddles several creative areas including ceramics, glass, furniture making, and foundry work with new technologies such as rapid prototyping, digitising and motion capture.

Contrary to Rashid's blobs, I believe Ron Arad has been a little more successful, certainly more successful critically and I think to a certain degree he has adopted the same or similar technologies to Rashid but perhaps has been a little more particular with whom he works. Certainly Arad received wide critical acclaim for his 'Not Hand Made' and 'Not Made in China' series of lights which were produced as part of a V&A exhibition a few years back using stereolithography technologies and I think his use of computers is generally found to be a success. Rashid and Arad are only two of the many contemporary designers that rely heavily on emerging computing and manufacturing technologies – the list is endless – Ross Lovegrove, Frank Gehry, Thomas Heatherwick, I could go on and on. Certainly within the 'PBB' exhibition, emerging computing and manufacturing technologies are being exploited beautifully in the work of Justin Marshall and his exploration of the use of digital technologies and craft practices and how these new forms of digital production might better support the development of more sustainable forms of craft practice.

To finish, I have listed a number of issues that design tutors, design researchers and design practitioners might want to consider. Do we wish to go down the path of the specialist or should we celebrate the generalist nature of designers? We must also consider what is meant by the terms 'local' and 'global' and think about where does design wish to go? There are many arguments for keeping design local and craft-based – most notably as recently posited by the great Ezio Manzini[4]. Designers are regularly encouraged and frequently have demands placed upon them to be flexible and have greater flexibility in their working practices. But just how much flexibility can designers be asked for? There are questions of intellectual capital versus craft ability and in recent years there has been an emphasis placed on the former to the detriment of the latter. We should be aware of prioritising knowledge over craft. Finally, many of the issues aforementioned have been reinforced in the recent Bureau for European Design Associations report (BEDA, 2004). This

report challenges the design profession, amongst other things, to explore how best designers can create environments to manipulate or utilise the new and emerging computing technologies in a creative way.

Dr. Paul Rodgers
Napier University
www.napier.ac.uk/sci/

Paul Rodgers is Reader in Design in the School of Creative Industries at Napier University, Edinburgh. Rodgers has published more than 90 book chapters, international journal and conference papers. This includes 'Inspiring Designers' (Black Dog Publishers, London, 2004) a major book on the "iconic influences" of successful designers throughout the world.

References

The Bureau of European Design Associations (BEDA) (2004) Design Issues in Europe Today, BEDA, Barcelona.
Coles, A. (2005) DesignArt, Tate Publishing, London.
Coles, A. (2007) Design and Art, The Whitechapel Gallery Publishers, London.
Flusser, V. (1999) The Shape of Things: A Philosophy of Design, Reaktion Books, London.
Guixé, M. (2002) 1:1 Martí Guixé, 010 Publishers, Rotterdam.
Hayon, J. (2007) Documents..., Icon, 47(May), p. 83 – 96.
Jones, W. (2007) Grayson Perry: Portrait of the Artist as a Young Girl, Vintage Publishers, London.
Paul, F. (2003) David Shrigley, Centre d'Art du Domaine de Kerguehennec, France.
Schouwenberg, L. (2003) Hella Jongerius, Phaidon Press, London.
Seymour, R. (2006) Heads or Tails?, Design Week, 21(36), p. 19.
West, D. (2007) A New Generation, Icon, 43(January), p. 56 – 64.

4 www.sustainable-everyday.net/manzini

Designing Digital Art

Digital art has always been characterised by boundary and discipline defying artworks and practitioners. It seemed in the late 20th Century that the new communication and Internet technologies would give rise to a final Avant-Garde and pervasive form of art (Rush, 1999) that would lead the mainstream art world to rethink and rewrite the history and context for contemporary practice. It is now several years later and digital/new media art is possibly having to face rethinking its own loosely held definitions. New media/digital art has been generally defined as art that not only incorporates computers and other emerging digital

(Carl Goodman in Jennings, 2000). However, this definition of new media has until recently somewhat obscured the history and development of digital practices that are hardware or object-based.

Digital sculpture is regularly limited to a few pages in most new media art publications (if it is mentioned at all). While artists making objects with rapid prototyping technology satisfy the definition above, their works in some cases have been criticised because the aesthetics owe too much to how the objects were made rather than what is being made and why. These works are routinely exhibited in their raw state which does not necessarily complement the subject being explored (Ganis, 2004). Produced in small editions or as one-offs many of these works also tend to deny their ability to be easily mass-produced, in order to conform to

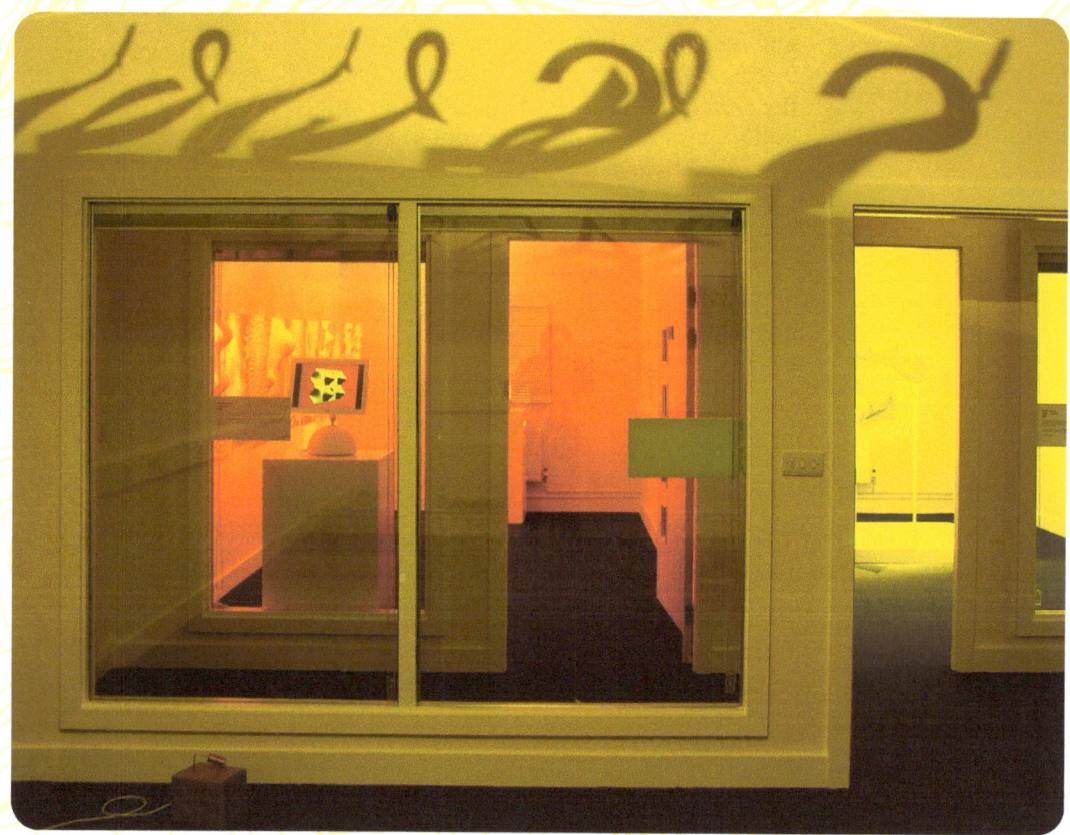

technologies but that also moulds and subverts the computational powers of the computer and technology to create new signs, meanings, communications and forms (Jennings, 2000). In other words it is digital art concerned with its 'digital-ness'

traditional, Western paradigms of art that still value the 'original'. Whilst Marcel Duchamp may have made it acceptable to question the role of authorship, individuality and originality within art, the impact of this has not always been easy to reconcile within the dominant models of contemporary practice, curation, criticism, policy and funding.

Nevertheless, the 'Perimeters, Boundaries and Borders' exhibition and symposium allowed the public to see works by practitioners from different disciplinary backgrounds that are repurposing these digital tools for their own ends. Geoffrey Mann, Simon Husslein, Nio Architecten, Justin Marshall, Tavs Jørgensen, Brit Bunkley, and FutureFactories, can all be considered as part of a new wave of makers that are producing designed objects that cross fluidly between commercial and cultural contexts within the 'creative industries'. For new media art this means that perhaps we are entering a period where the technological object is as important as the digital image. If this is the case, we are in need of a more expansive definition of new media art which includes not only the conceptual and technical history of computing, histories of representation and histories of communication (Lister, Dovey, Giddings, Grant and Kelly, 2003 p. 52) – but also histories of fabrication (Marshall, 2008).

The 'PBB' exhibition also engaged with and contributed to the discussions around 'Device Art'. Originally presented by Machiko Kusahara (2006) this category of work covers a range of practices emerging out of Japan that integrates not only art and technology, but also design, entertainment and popular culture. Kusahara explains that within Japan, cultural and historical distinctions between fine and applied art were never made. Central to understanding or characterising 'Device Art' is that it often takes a playful and positive approach to technology where the boundaries between high and low-art are less rigid than in the West. Kusahara theorises that in Europe and the United States, we have been unable to overcome a deep-rooted mistrust of technology and automation - seeing it as a de-humanising force, and that this sensibility pervades much of new media art practice and the critical discourse surrounding it. While this may be evident in the concerns of late 20th Century Western culture and therefore its art forms, it has not always been the case elsewhere. Seen from a cyclical point of view (or one where we are constantly moving between convergent and divergent forces) Western art has enjoyed periods where little or no distinction between the fine and applied arts was made - such as in the historical Avant-Gardes. These movements often embraced new developments in the science and technology of the day for progressive, radical, political, material and aesthetic ends.

Perhaps 'Device Art' is merely indicative of the latest phase within a technological adoption cycle – having more to do with the pervasiveness of physical computing, prevalence of networked devices, and the intersections taking place between design, craft, architecture and art via computer-based design and fabrication tools (Marshall, 2008). Certainly within 'PBB' there are a number of works that can be looked at within the framework of 'Device Art', such as Ben Woodeson's "Chicken Soup from Mars" and Aoife Ludlow's "Remember to Forget?". With "Remember to Forget?" we are asked to consider the taken for granted interactions we have with everyday objects and through technology we are able to remove these actions from the unconscious. Simon Blackmore's "LSD Drive" takes the mantra of environmentalism (reduce, reuse, and recycle) into the technological arena with re-appropriate, re-mediate, and re-assemble. These works all provide a kind of voice for the objects providing feedback between themselves, their users and the environment. For a new media art exhibition 'PBB' included very little conventionally interactive art, instead it focused on creating subtle sensory interactions. "Ibuki – Presence in a Sigh" by Tabei and Miyauchi, is a work which invites the user to hear sound through the body. This work doesn't subvert the technology but rather uses it to subvert our understanding of the senses.

Public art has long included artists utilising projected images, slideshows, video, neon, lasers and sound in their works. They have been used to transform, both physically and conceptually, a variety of spaces whether as enhancements, interventions or augmentations. In common with new media art, public art discourse has centred on changing/ challenging the relationship between subject, object, viewer and site – removing it from the constraints and confines of the institution. With "Wifi Camera Obscura" Somlai-Fisher, Sjölén and Haque have created a work that operates somewhere between public art and gallery-based work, between 'Device Art' and data visualisation in order to make apparent the electro-magnetic space of wifi networks. Baily and Corby are also exploring the phenomenological and the ephemeral through their work "Cyclone.soc". By mapping live conversations in newsgroups onto weather patterns, the audience can interact with and interpolate changes in a discussion thread. Net art has always made use of the proliferation of information and data available on the web. It has also pushed the boundaries of interactivity and communication technologies. In "What's Cooking Grandma", Human Beans have created a work for the exhibition that harnesses the creative possibilities of web 2.0. If public art is art in, about, and for the public realm, then this new type of net art gives the public the power to make art by, for and about themselves in a networked and distributed space.

The 'PBB' exhibition and symposium attempted to create a snapshot of shifting terrains within new media art practice. This exhibition was not so much a treatise on what's next - in fact, in many ways it is very unconcerned with the new. Instead we attempted to conceive of an exhibition where different trajectories of art and technology practice and critical discourses could come together. 'PBB' created a framework that transcended existing disciplinary, cultural and contextual paradigms in order to come up with - not answers, but new questions.

Cezanne Charles
Board Member and Co-curator
www.fastuk.org.uk

Cezanne Charles is an artist, curator and arts executive. She is committed to exploring interaction, participation and co-creation strategies that involve and engage audiences as participants. She is currently the Creative Industries Director for ArtServe Michigan and is the former Executive Director of New Media Scotland (2004-2007). Since 1998, Charles has worked within rootoftwo (a hybrid art and design practice with John Marshall). rootoftwo's works generate unconventional spatial and temporal relations between maker, site, work and audience. rootoftwo has exhibited in the US, Europe, Australia and online. In addition to her work with Fast-uk, Charles also curates exhibitions and urban screenings with other artist-led groups such as Video In the Built Environment (v1b3) and artcore and is a member of the Upgrade! International network.

References

Rush, M. (1999) New Media in Late 20th Century Art, Thames and Hudson, London. p. 8.
Jennings, P. (2000). New Media Arts | New Funding Models commissioned report for the Rockefeller Foundation Creativity and Culture Program. New York. p. 1-2.
Ganis, W. (2004) Digital Sculpture: Ars Ex Machina, Sculpture Magazine vol.23, no.8, Washington, DC.
Lister, Dovey, Giddings, Grant, and Kelly (2003) New Media: A Critical Introduction, Routledge, London. p. 52.
Marshall, J. (2008) An Exploration of Hybrid Art and Design Practice Using Computer-based Design and Fabrication Tools, The Robert Gordon University, Aberdeen. p. 18.
Kusahara, M. (2006) Device Art: A New Form of Media Art from a Japanese Perspective, Intelligent Agent, vol.6, no.2, New York.

GROUND FLOOR

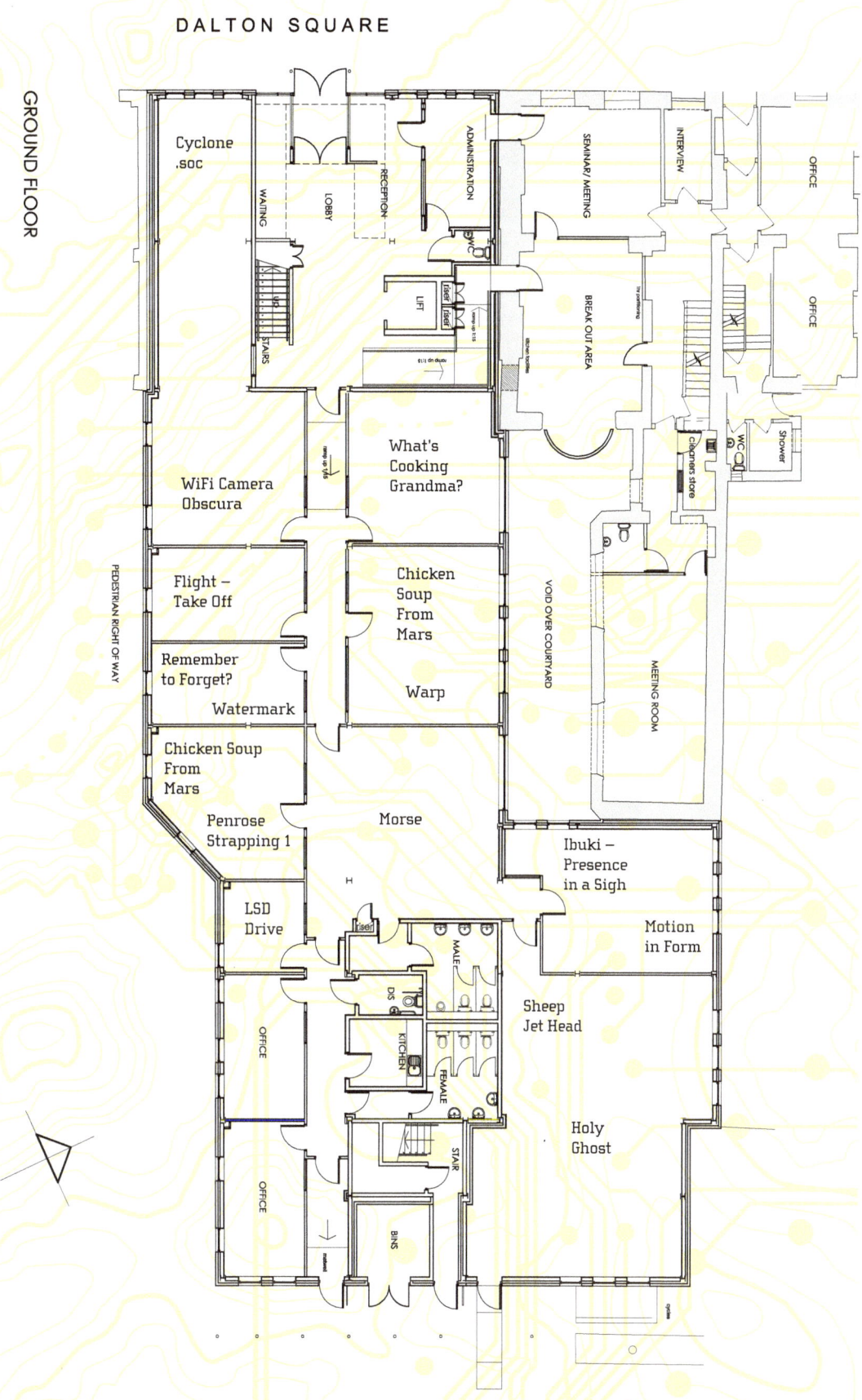

Cyclone .soc

WAITING

LOBBY

RECEPTION

ADMINISTRATION

SEMINAR / MEETING

INTERVIEW

OFFICE

OFFICE

LIFT

STAIRS

LIFT

BREAK OUT AREA

WiFi Camera Obscura

What's Cooking Grandma?

Flight – Take Off

Chicken Soup From Mars

Remember to Forget?

Watermark

Warp

VOID OVER COURTYARD

MEETING ROOM

Chicken Soup From Mars

Penrose Strapping 1

Morse

Cleaners store

WC

Shower

Ibuki – Presence in a Sigh

LSD Drive

Motion in Form

OFFICE

MALE

DIS

KITCHEN

FEMALE

Sheep Jet Head

Holy Ghost

PEDESTRIAN RIGHT OF WAY

OFFICE

STAIR

BINS

CityLab, Dalton Square, Lancaster, U.K.

Cyclone.soc

Gavin Baily & Tom Corby

Cyclone.soc is a projected installation that brings together two contemporary phenomena: severe weather and the polarised nature of debate that occurs in some online newsgroup forums.

The project maps live conversations from political and religious newsgroups onto the isobars of hurricanes and the complex structure of the weather is used to visualise the churn and eddies of newsgroup debate. Cyclone.soc is a navigable environment that gives the user the ability to zoom in or out and skate across and through the cyclonic weather formations in order to read or be immersed in the newsgroup text.

Gavin Baily's work has focused on developing conjunctions of software-based visualisation and the data traces of social processes.

Tom Corby is interested in the development of innovative concepts, and processes that relocate the digital image within wider aesthetic and critical frameworks.

www.reconnoitre.net

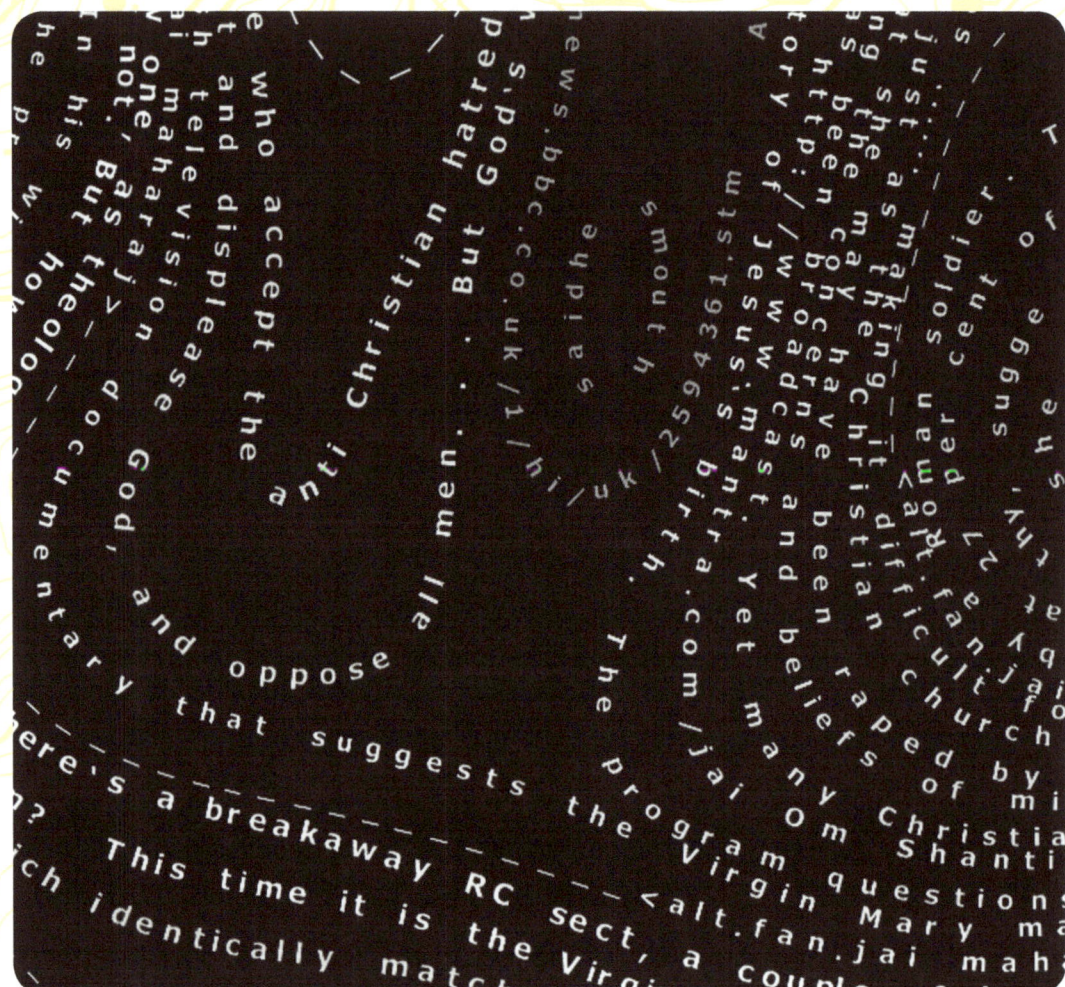

Cyclone.soc (detail)
Gavin Baily & Tom Corby,
2006.

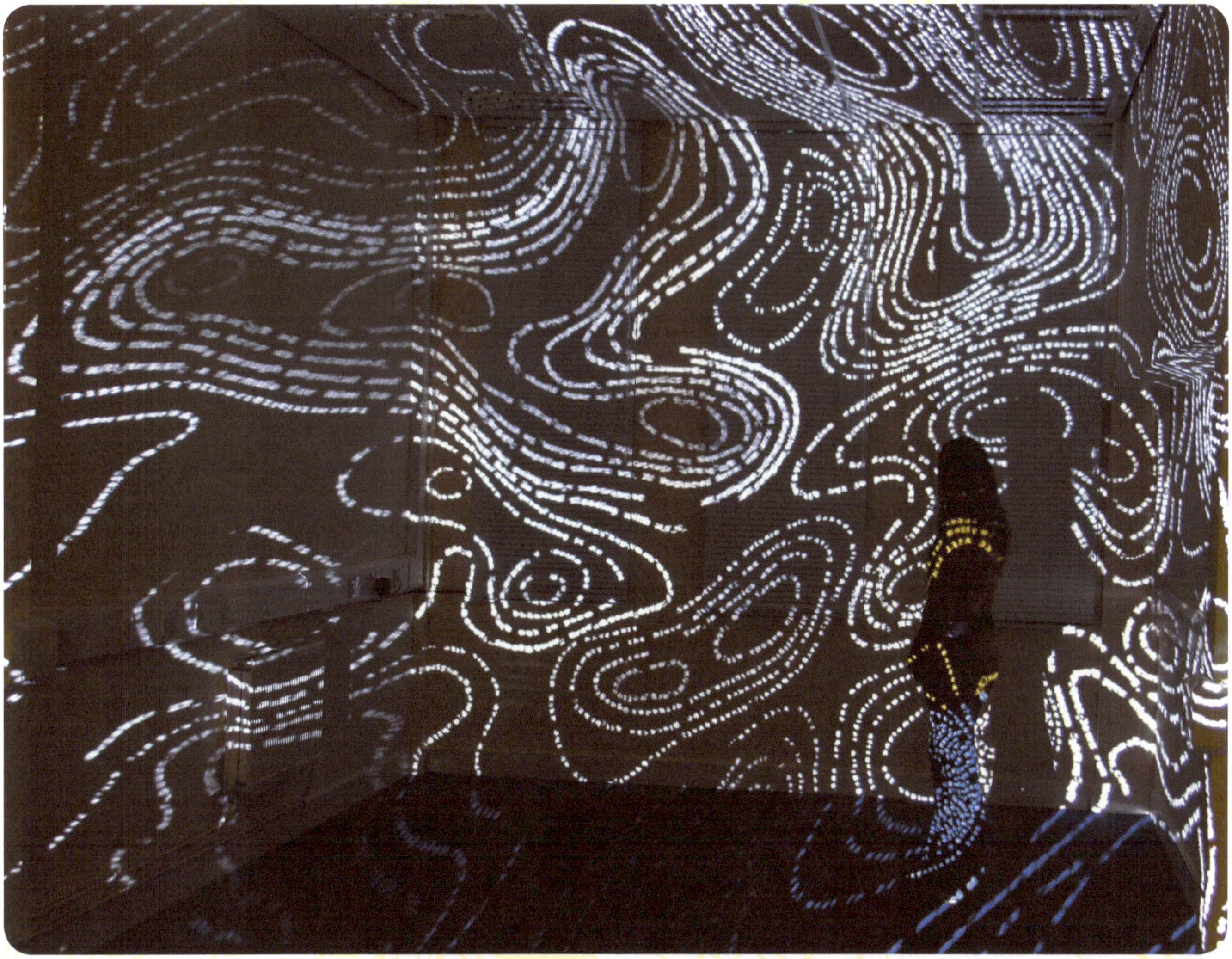

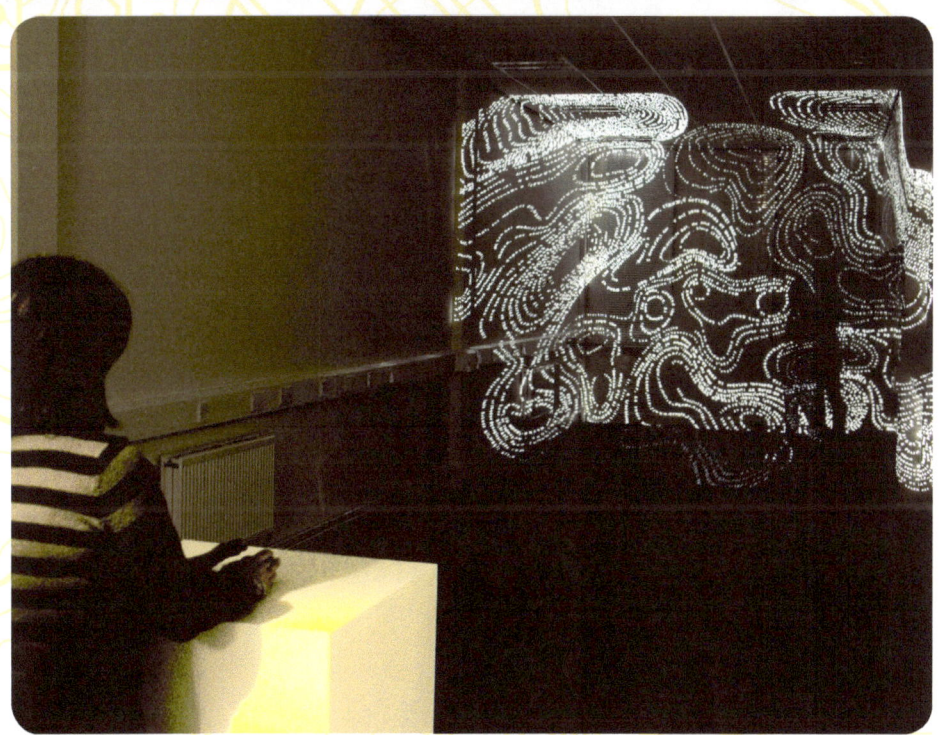

Cyclone.soc

Gavin Baily & Tom Corby, 2006.

Cyclone.soc is a navigable environment that gives the user the ability to be immersed in newsgroup text. These conversations 'condense' in the work's environment.

Cyclone.soc uses edited data from different storms derived from publicly available satellite forecasting for the Eastern coast of the United States.

WiFi Camera Obscura

Adam Somlai-Fischer, Bengt Sjölén & Usman Haque

An interpretation of the traditional camera obscura that uses an antenna fabricated from empty cans of wasabi- covered peas. This is mounted on a robotic head that scans for wireless network signals. The results are presented on a nearby screen as constantly updating images.

Adam Somlai-Fischer is an architect and interaction researcher. As a founding partner of Aether Architecture he specialises in designing interactive architectural projects.

Bengt Sjölén is an independent game technology researcher.

Usman Haque has been a researcher at the Interaction Design Institute Ivrea, Italy; artist-in-residence at the International Academy of Media Arts and Sciences, Japan; and has also worked in the US, UK and Malaysia. Until 2005 he was a teacher in the Interactive Architecture Workshop at the Bartlett School of Architecture, London.

www.aether.hu
www.automata.se
www.haque.co.uk

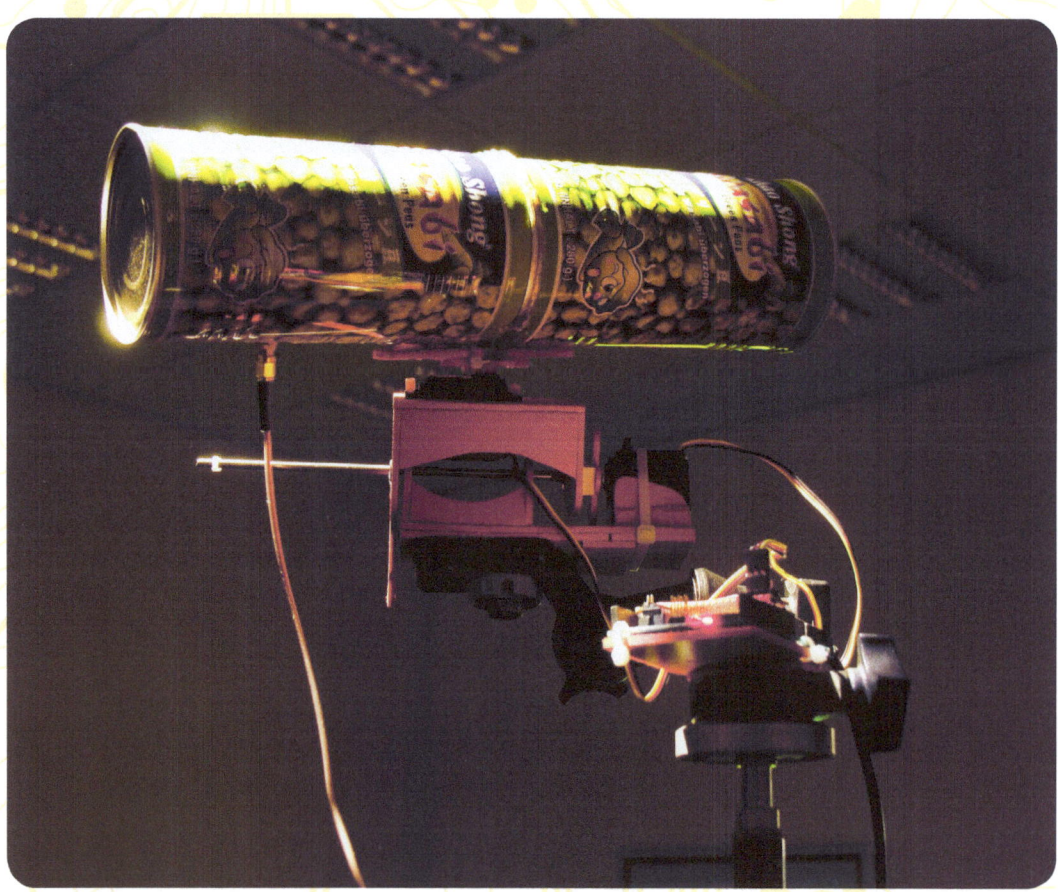

WiFi Camera Obscura
Adam Somlai-Fischer,
Bengt Sjölén & Usman
Haque, 2006.

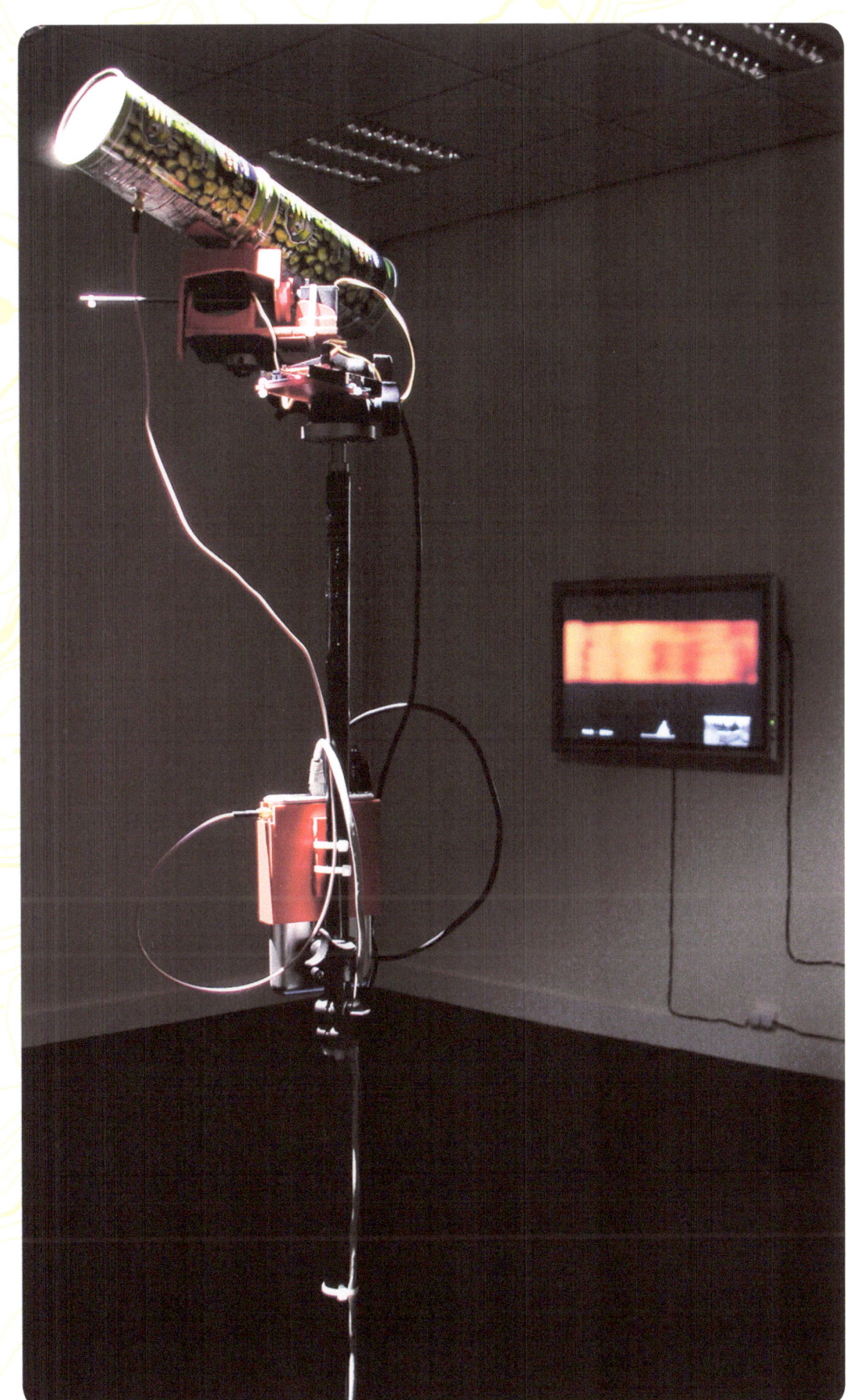

WiFi Camera Obscura

Adam Somlai-Fischer, Bengt Sjölén & Usman Haque, 2006.

In the age of "enlightenment", electromagnetic waves as "visible light" formed our most ubiquitous medium. Today, we are increasingly creating and responding to nonvisual electromagnetic fields - those emanating from our devices and environments.

This project takes realtime "photos" of the electromagnetic space of wifi networks. These are increasingly found in coffee shops, offices and homes throughout the developed world.

What's Cooking Grandma?

Human Beans

Imagine being able to view videos of the grandmothers' of the world sharing the recipes and techniques they've spent their lives perfecting. Human Beans aim to popularise a new genre of documentary video clip - the 'Grandma Recipe'. They want to catalyse the mass documentation of Grandmothers' cooking their special recipes in their own kitchens.

Human Beans are encouraging people to upload their own videos to:
www.whatscookinggrandma.net

Alongside these films are prototype 'Grandma Players' - a new kitchen appliance (based on a modified jam jar). These are designed to record Grandma's instructions and the sound of her cooking - so you can play her back in your own kitchen and cook along with Grandma .

Human Beans create provocative concepts. They make fictional products by hacking commercial culture and design new services by working with real people. Their work is disseminated through spam, media, shop shelves and exhibitions. Human Beans is a collaboration between advertising creative and designer Mickael Charbonnel and design strategist Chris Vanstone. Their work was recently included in the 'HearWear' exhibition at the V&A, London and 'Design and the Elastic Mind' at MoMA, New York.

www.whatscookinggrandma.net
www.humanbeans.net

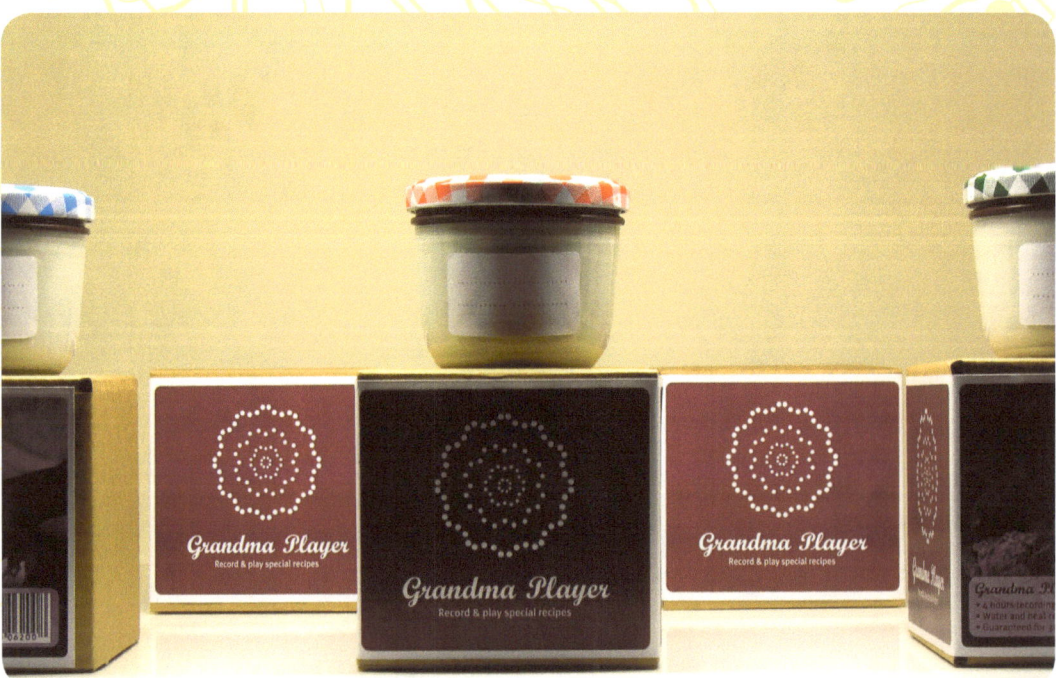

What's Cooking Grandma?
Human Beans, 2006.

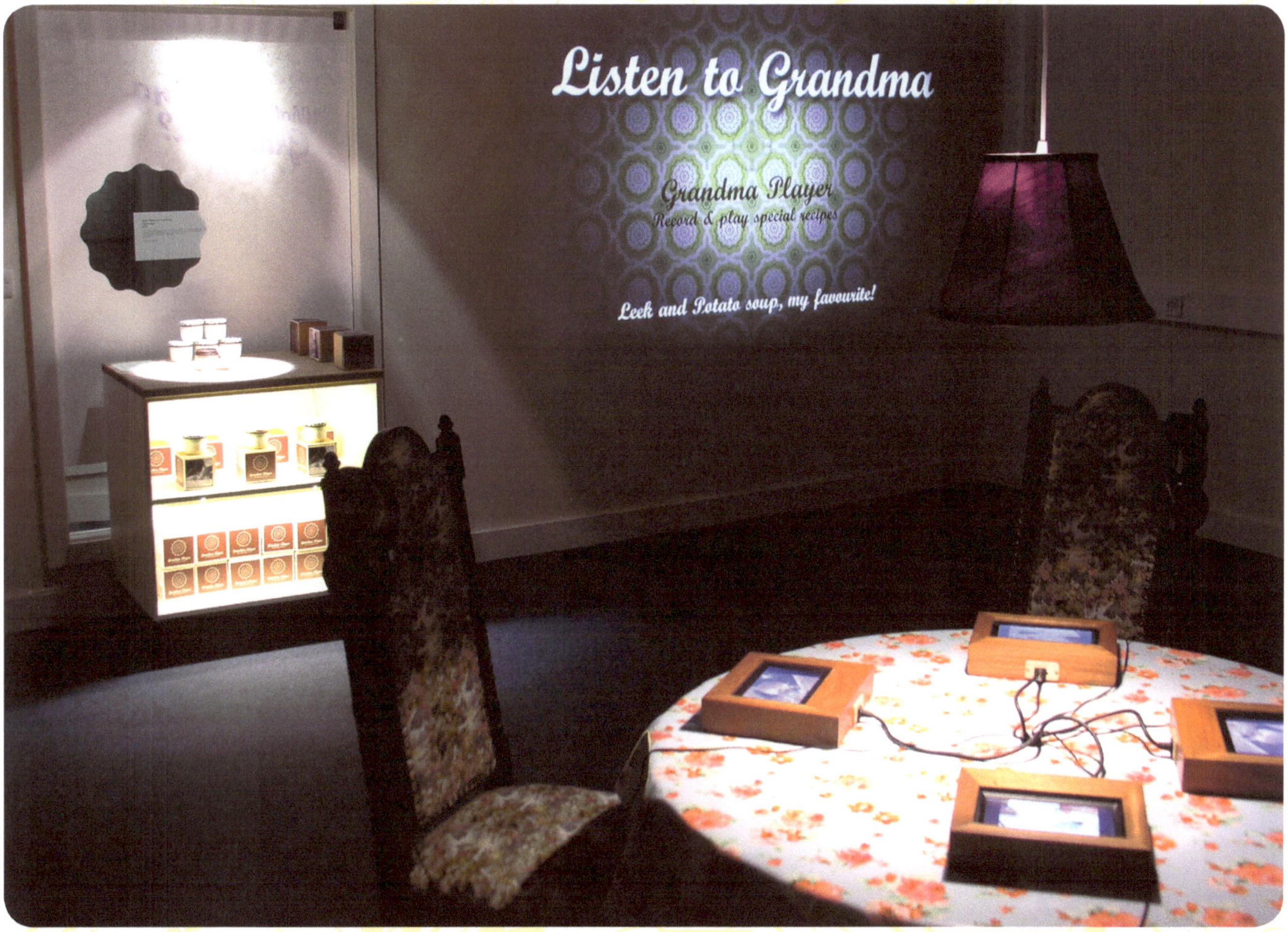

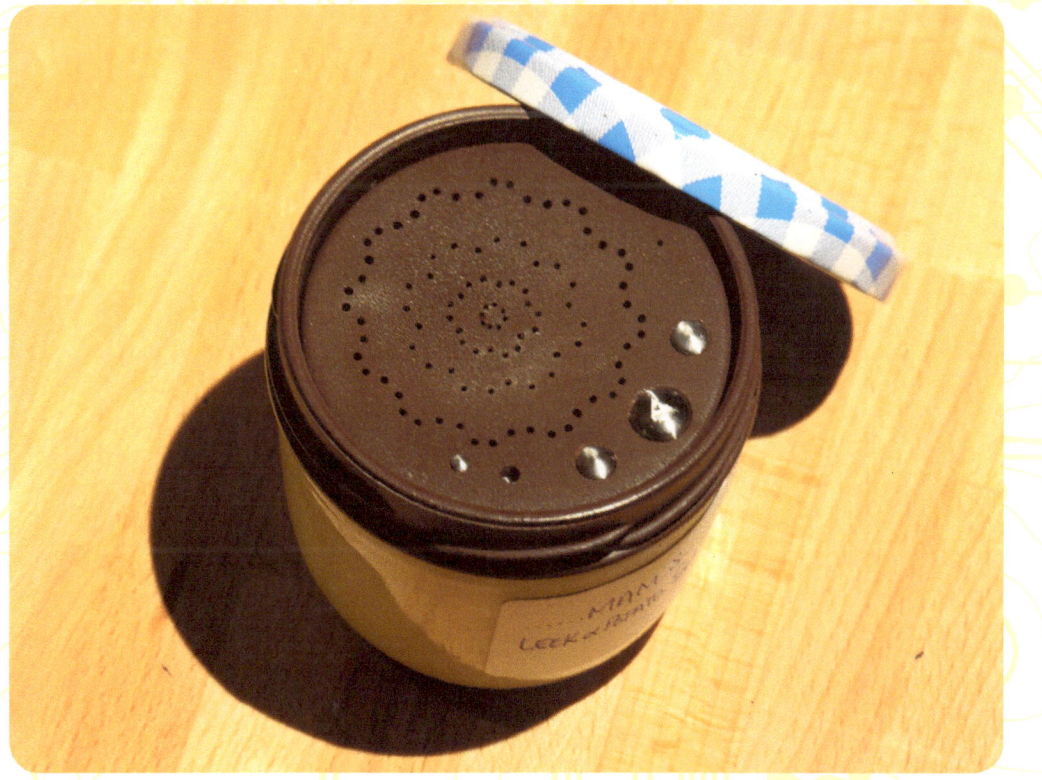

What's Cooking Grandma?

Human Beans, 2006.

Technologies which were once bleeding-edge and the domain of professionals are now commonplace and affordable. This democratisation of technology is fuelling the development of new forms of literacy. In this project Human Beans explore the potential to connect the last generation of British women who stayed at home and cooked for their families with the YouTube generation. In creating a new genre of video clip, they want to leverage the potential for self-produced media content of cultural significance.

Flight – Take Off

Geoffrey Mann

Mann aspires to the impossible - the materialisation of the immaterial into a solid, permanent state. Flight – Take Off transforms the intangible flight path of a bird into a tangible object - a frozen moment in time. Five seconds each of the take off and landing of the bird have been captured by StroMotion™ technology. This is based on stroboscoping (a means of analysing rapid movement) so that the bird is perceived as a series of static images along its trajectory. Mann has then, frame-by-frame combined these 2D images into a virtual 3D surface. These objects were fabricated from this data through 3D printing technology.

Mann trained in 3D Design at Gray's School of Art in Aberdeen and studied Ceramics & Glass at the Royal College of Art, London. He works as product artist, digital consultant and lecturer and his current research focuses on creative ways of 'humanising' the processes of digital production.

Mann recently exhibited in 'Design and the Elastic Mind' at MoMA, New York. He was also a finalist for the Bombay Sapphire Prize, 2008.

www.mrmann.co.uk

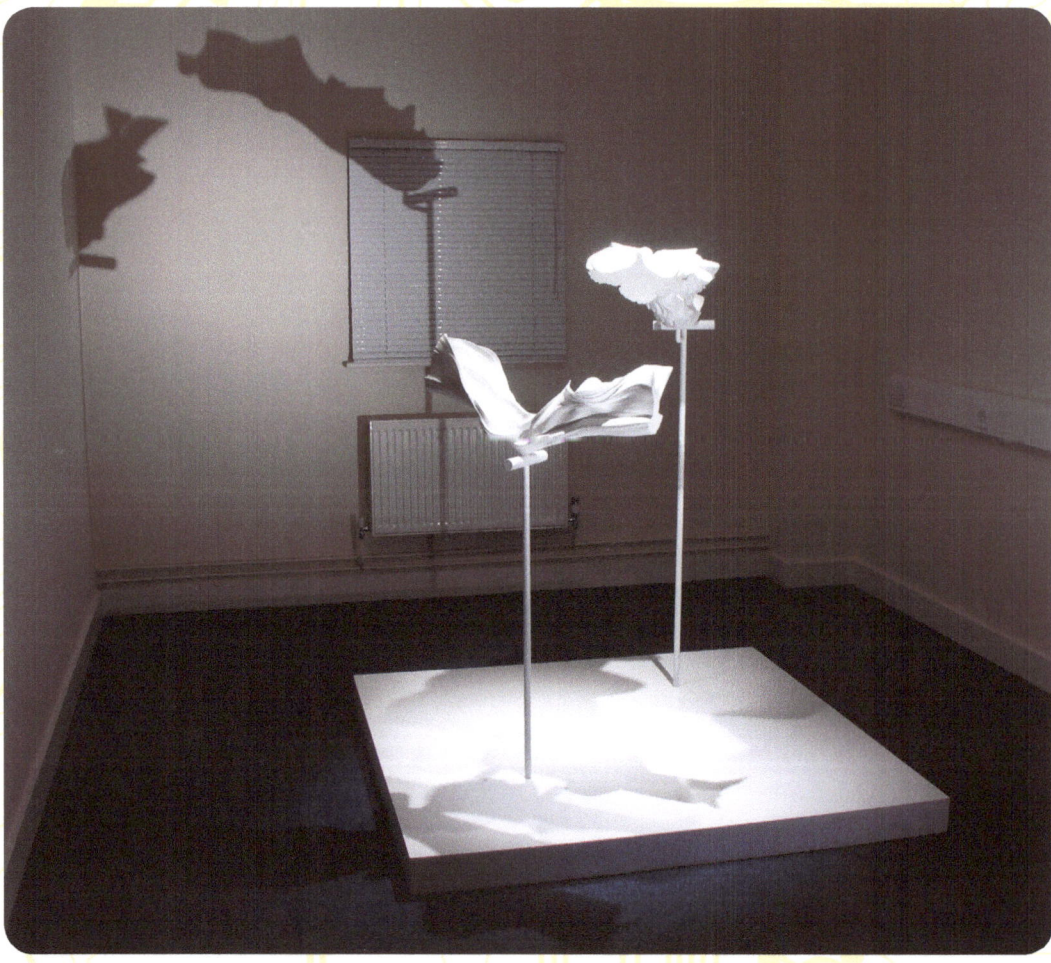

Flight – Take Off
Geoffrey Mann, 2006.

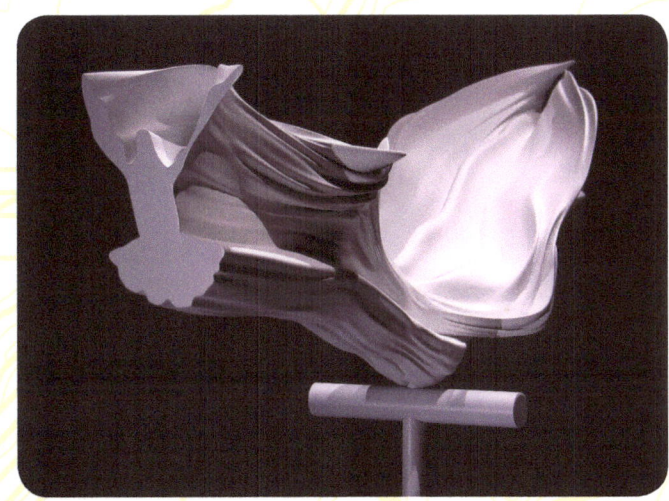

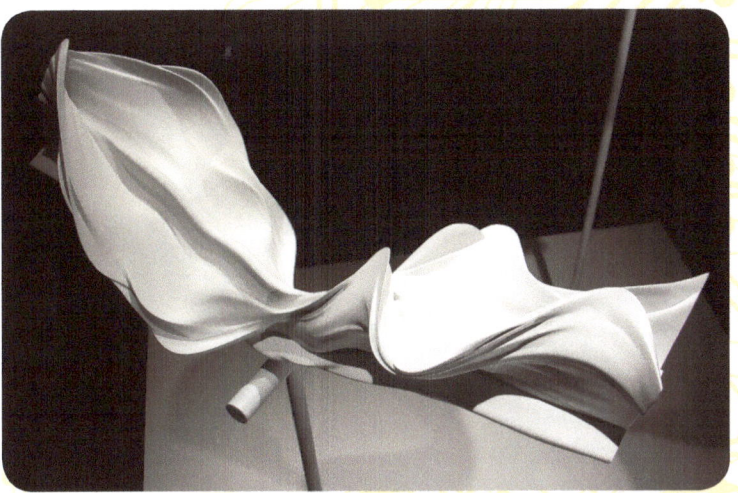

Flight – Take Off

Geoffrey Mann, 2006.

These objects have been made by a 3D printing process. The 3D Printer spreads out a thin layer of gypsum powder. An ink-jet print head prints an adhesive binder in the cross-section of the part being created. Between layers the build piston drops down, making room for the next layer. The process is repeated and each successive layer is bonded by the adhesive applied from the printhead. Once the part is finished, it is surrounded and supported by the compacted powder, which can be shaken loose from the finished part. The part is strengthened by dipping or coating with a sealant.

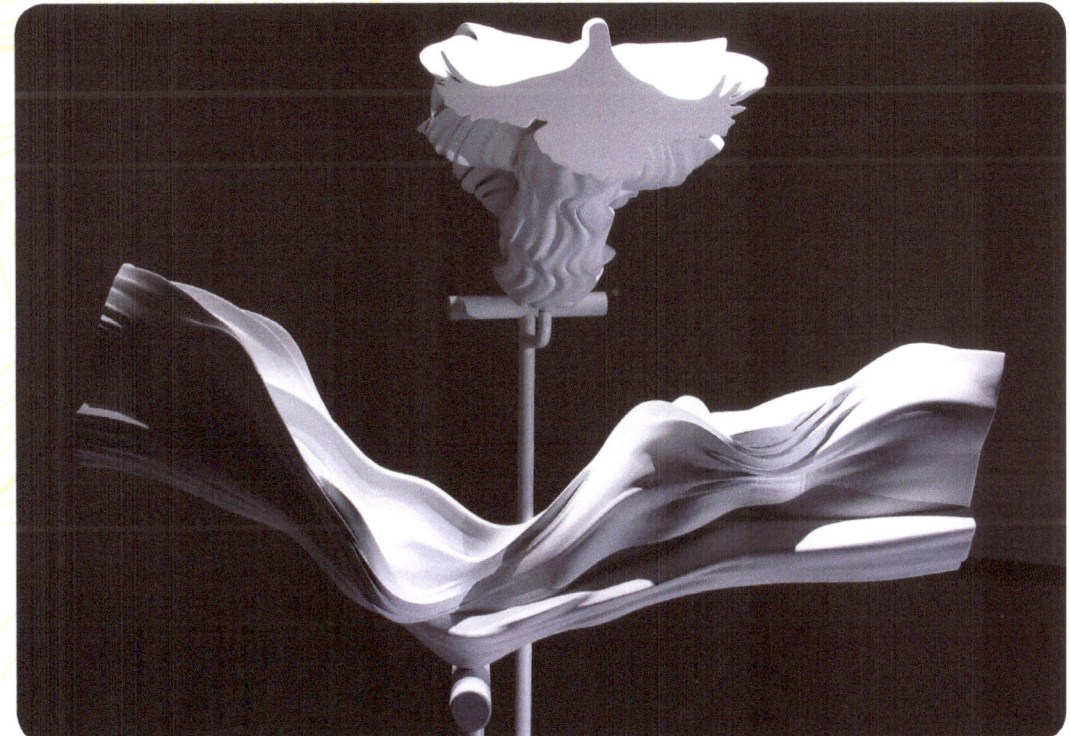

Warp

Simon Husslein

This rotating timepiece was originally designed for the six-storey rotunda of the Great Eastern Hotel, London. Its protruding warped forms, built by digital manufacturing, cast upright shadows of numbers to tell the time when each form is aligned with the light.

Husslein has worked on product design, interfaces, digital fonts, timepieces and furniture and now brings these diverse influences and practices together as a creative designer. He has designed for offices in Munich, Frankfurt and Tokyo. Working with Hannes Wettstein in Zurich, he managed projects for clients like BMW, Panasonic and Sony.

www.husslein.net

Diameter: 120cm

Height: 15cm

Total Weight: 3kg

Voltage: 240 V, 100 W

Mechanism: one rotation of the numbers per day

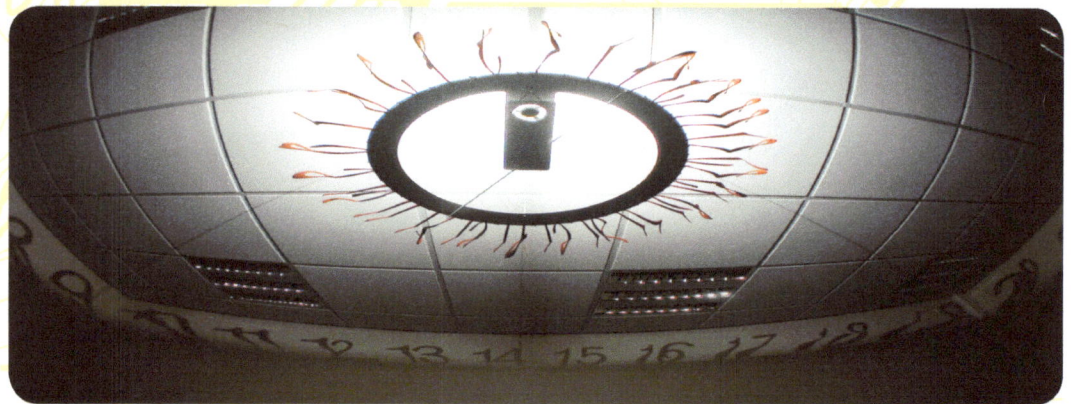

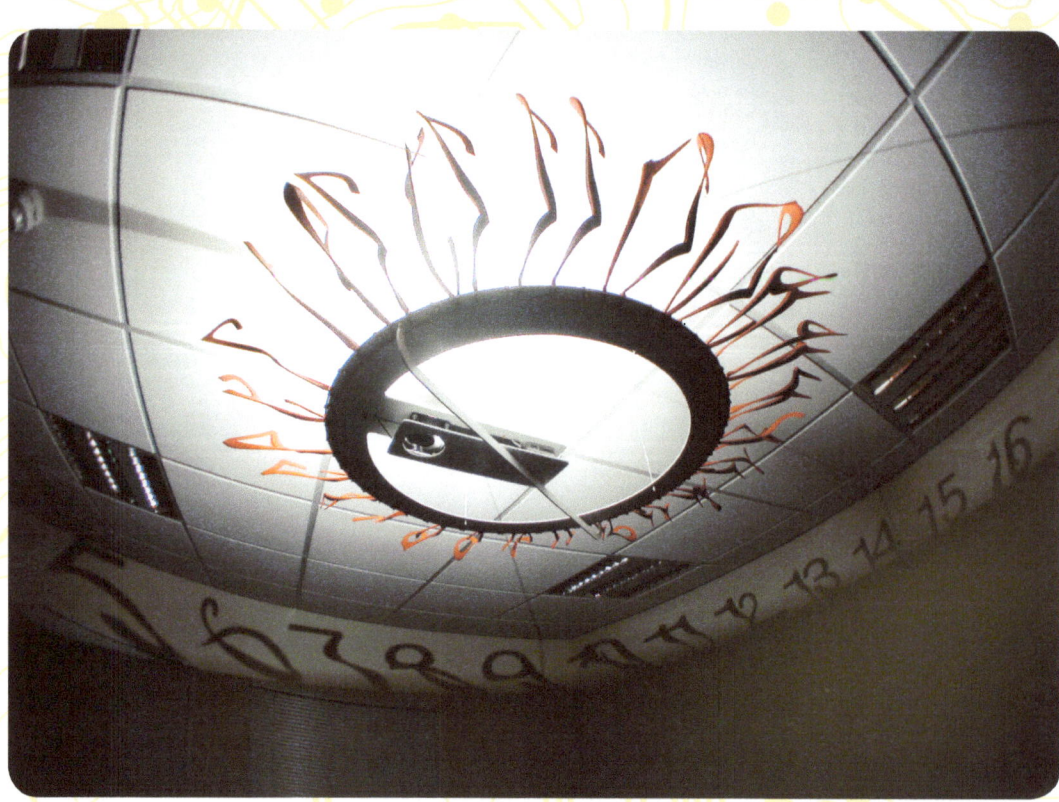

Warp
Simon Husslein, 2006.

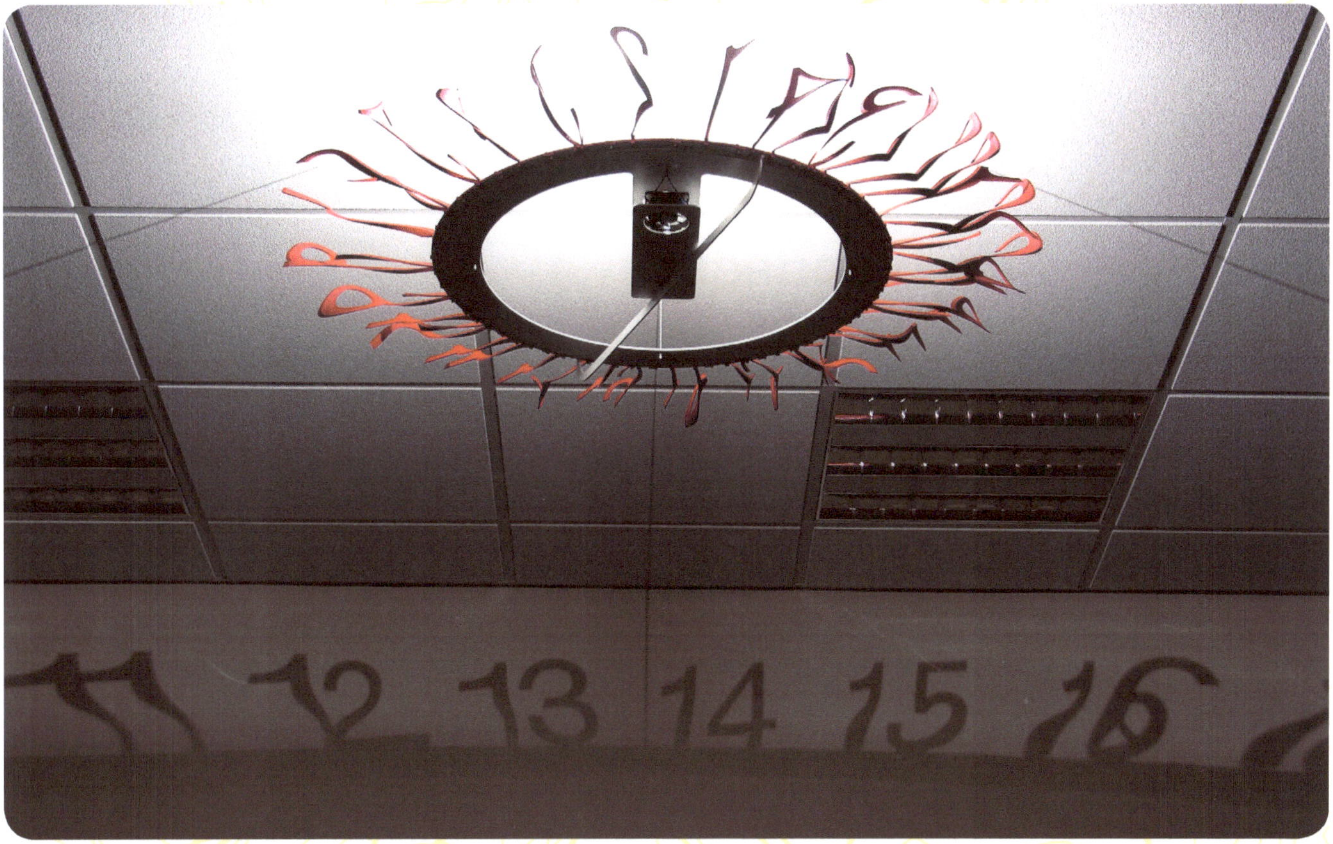

Warp

Simon Husslein, 2006.

The numbers are fabricated by the Selective Laser Sintering (SLS) process. This is an additive rapid manufacturing (RM) technique that uses a high power CO_2 laser to fuse small particles of plastic, metal, or ceramic powders into a mass representing a desired 3D object. The laser selectively fuses powdered material by scanning cross-sections generated from a 3D digital description of the part on the surface of a powder bed. After each cross-section is scanned, the powder bed is lowered by one layer thickness, a new layer of material is applied on top, and the process is repeated until the part is completed.

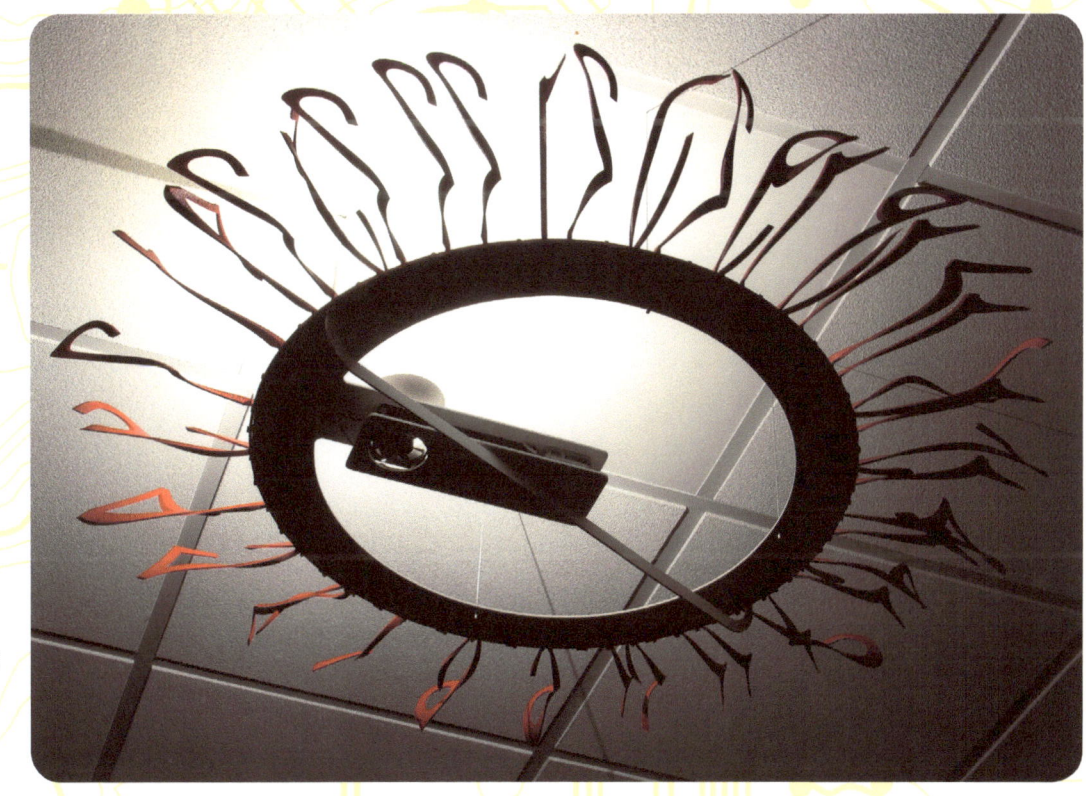

Chicken Soup From Mars

Ben Woodeson

Fourteen pairs of handmade electro-magnets placed throughout the exhibition that tap out Morse Code texts from or about self-help manuals with titles such as 'A Guide To Getting', 'Confidence, Trust and Loving' and 'Grow Rich'.

Different quantities of delay are programmed into each pair of magnets resulting in a random sonic landscape. The piece reflects Woodeson's ongoing interest in technology, communication and how we treat and/or trust information.

Born in London, Ben Woodeson studied at Chelsea College of Art and Glasgow School of Art. His other interests include CCTV, voice activated transmitters, bugs, surveillance, conservation of energy, form following function, information systems, information delivery, subversion, reinvention, wire as vehicle, manifestation and transference of energy, radio and sound.

www.woodeson.co.uk

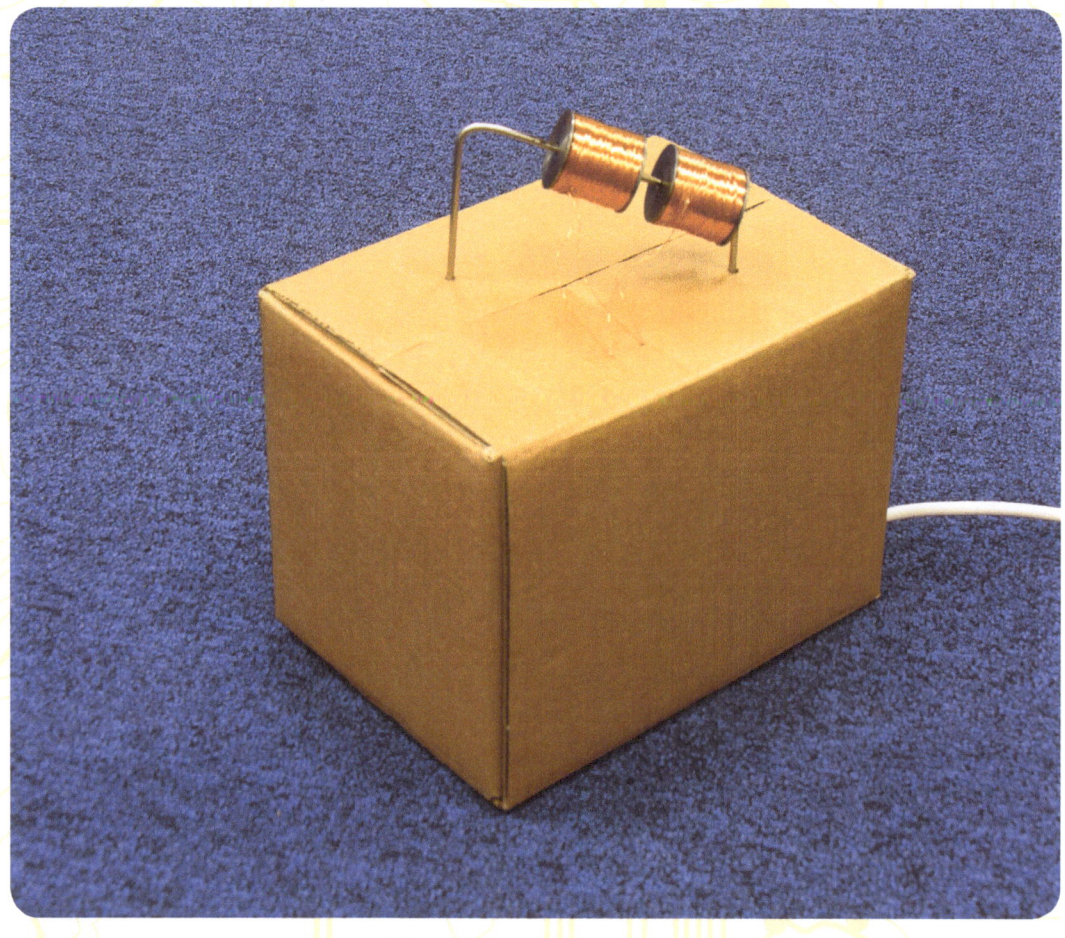

Chicken Soup From Mars
Ben Woodeson, 2006.

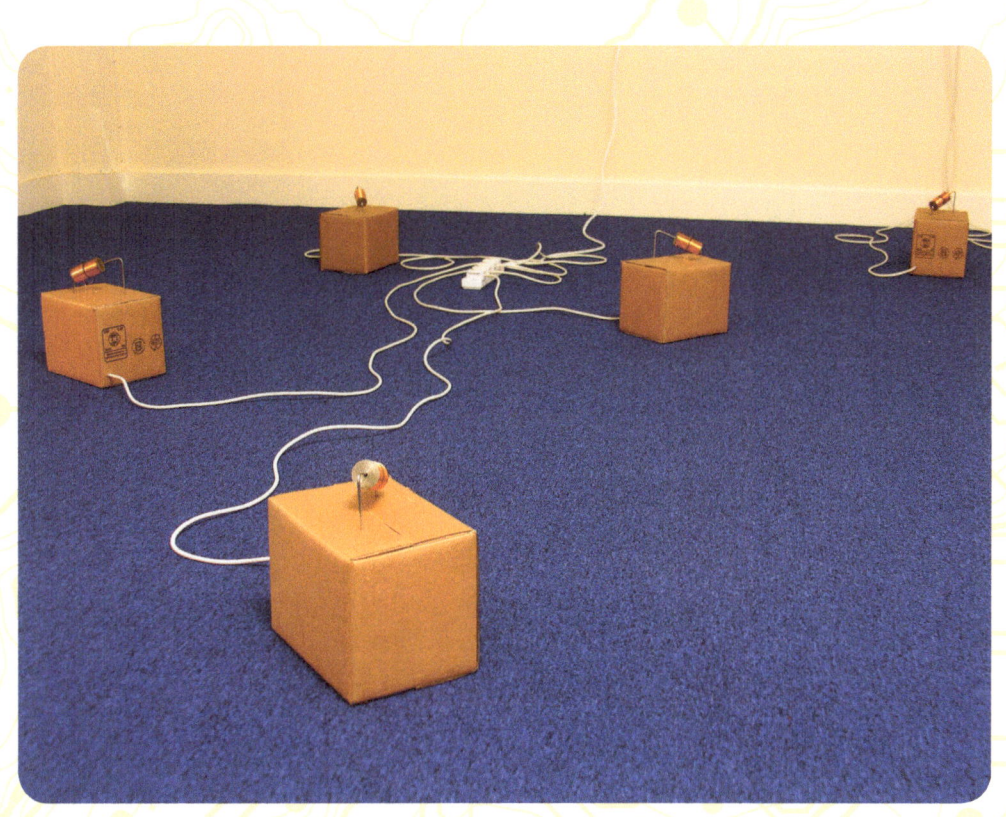

Chicken Soup From Mars
Ben Woodeson, 2006.

Chicken Soup From Mars is an installation that consists of up to fourteen separate but related pieces. Each individual work contains a pair of hand made electromagnets that tap out Morse code texts from or about self-help manuals. The individually titled works combine to form Chicken Soup From Mars.

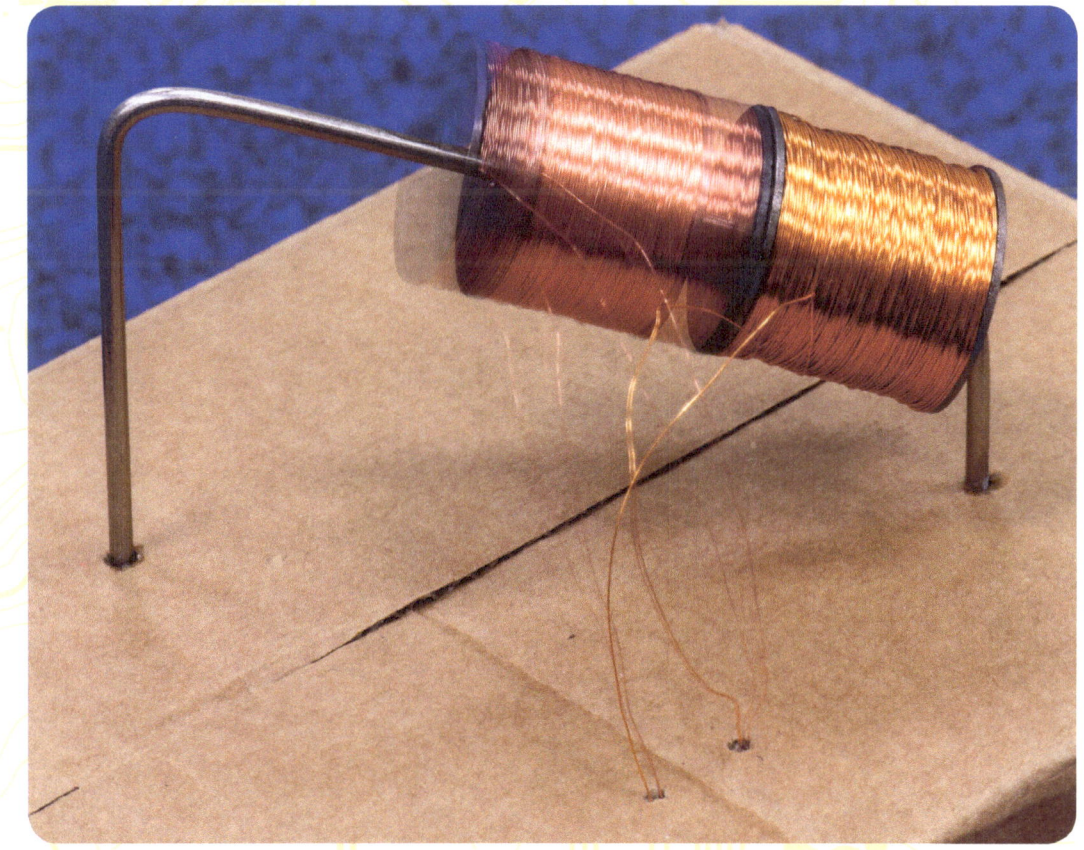

Watermark

NIO Architecten

Watermark is a series of prototype façade panels for a cluster of buildings with divergent functions: a music hall, a national soccer museum, a fast food restaurant, a school, a wellness center and several outdoor activity shops for Middelburg, a Dutch city close to the sea.

The panels are embodiments of moods that relate to leisure, crossed with various different characteristics of water: desire-whirl, arousal-cohesion, thrill-humidity, satisfaction-drop, curiosity-drifting, relaxation-rain, joy-floating, excitement-boiling, welcoming-wave, anticipation-ripple.

NIO Architecten is a design studio, set up by Maurice Nio and since 2003 also led by Joan Almekinders. Both graduated as architects from the Faculty of Architecture of the Delft University of Technology.

www.nio.nl

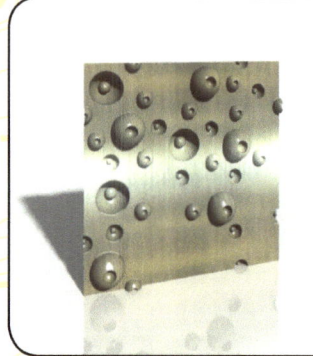 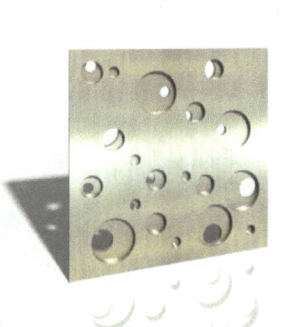 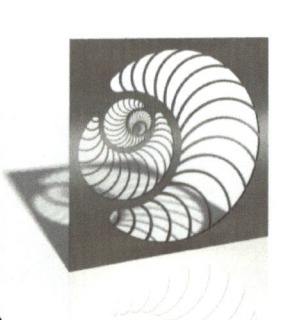

Watermark (renderings)
NIO Architecten, 2006.

Watermark
NIO Architecten, 2006.

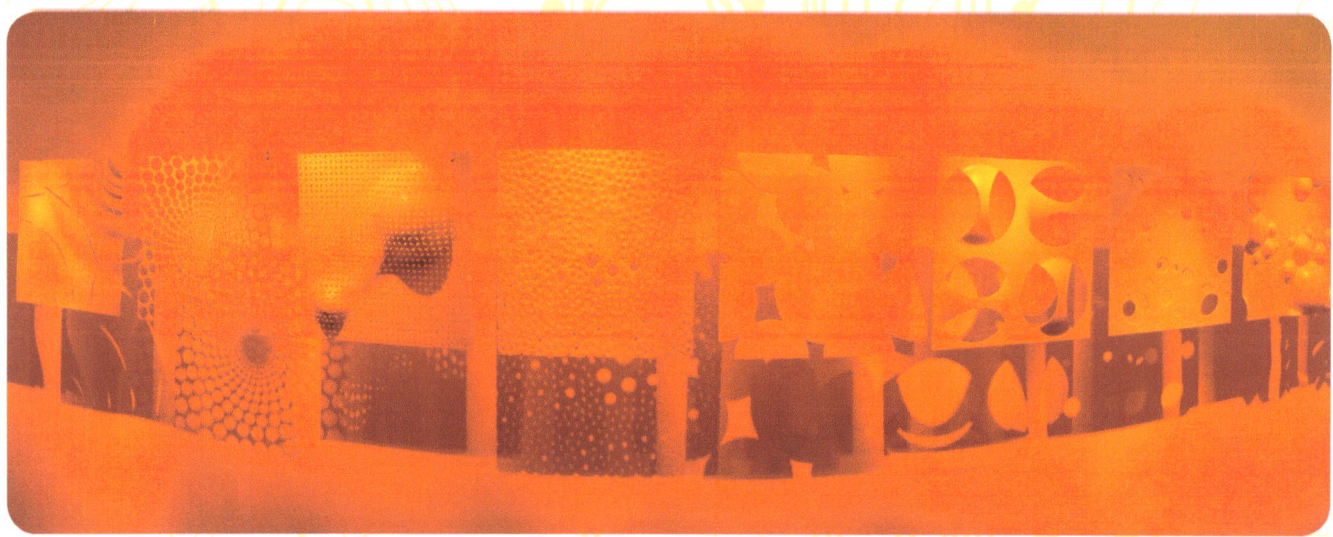

Watermark

NIO Architecten, 2006.

Every project starts with a set of hard facts, such as a client, a site, a budget and a program. Every project also starts for these architects with a search for a 'key' reference that is able to be absorbed by and influence the project. This project is located in an area of the Netherlands that is very much determined by natural elements, such as wind, sea and clay. The chosen 'key' in this case is 'the wave and the whirlwind'.

The architects have developed a set of rules, related to a building material where circles will be expressed in several ways. These could be small round perforations in a steel plate, patterns in concrete, big round constructional elements. For this exhibition they present several rapid prototypes of building materials that will be used within the project.

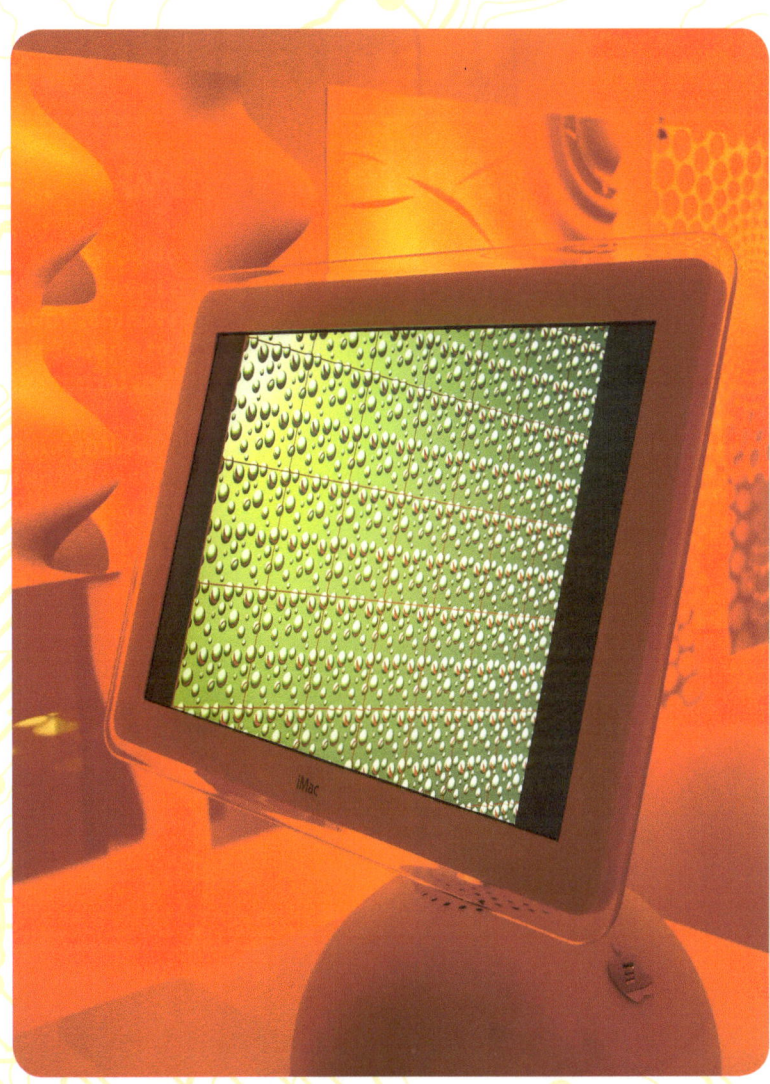

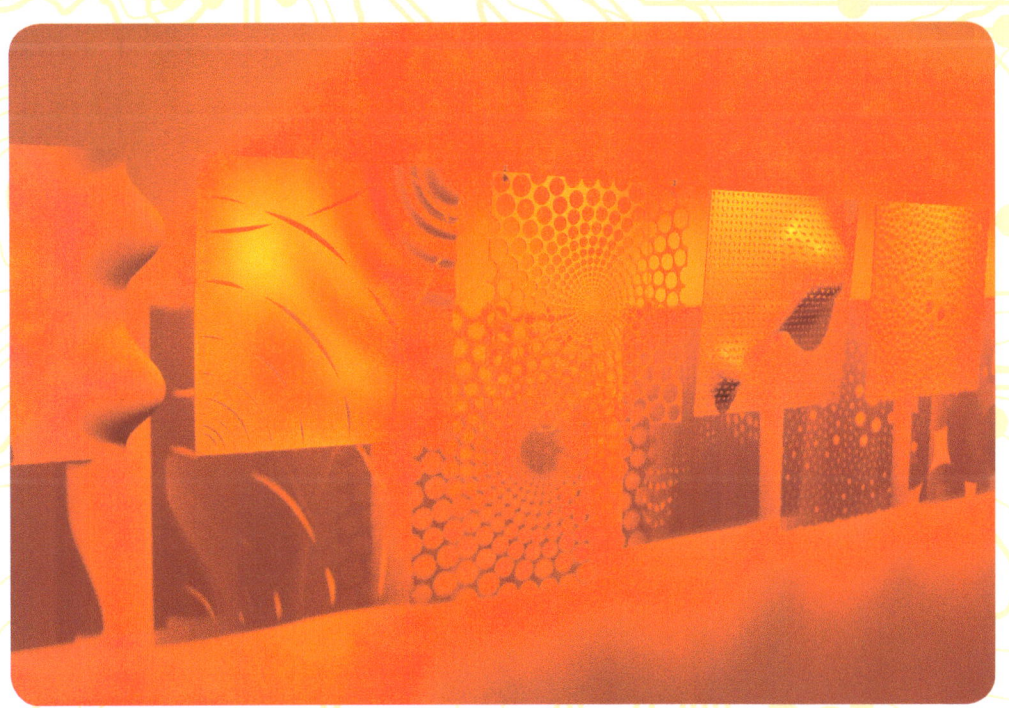

Remember to Forget?

Aoife Ludlow

Interactions with jewellery objects while they are being worn are often sub-conscious or habit-related. As such, often the most conscious interaction occurs at the point of putting on or taking off the jewellery, rather than whilst it is being worn. Remember to Forget? proposes conceptual designs for jewellery pieces, which contain RFID (radio frequency identity) tags and other hidden technology.

The jewellery box tracks and records when and how long the piece is worn for, based on the time it is absent from its place in the box. The more the piece is worn the brighter the glow from the box, the less the piece is worn the darker the box becomes, gradually fading into the background. This information could be a reassuring reflection of significance or a reminder that it is time to change some habits.

Ludlow is based in Belfast, Northern Ireland and works as Research Assistant at Interface: Research in Art, Technologies and Design.

www.aoifestuff.com

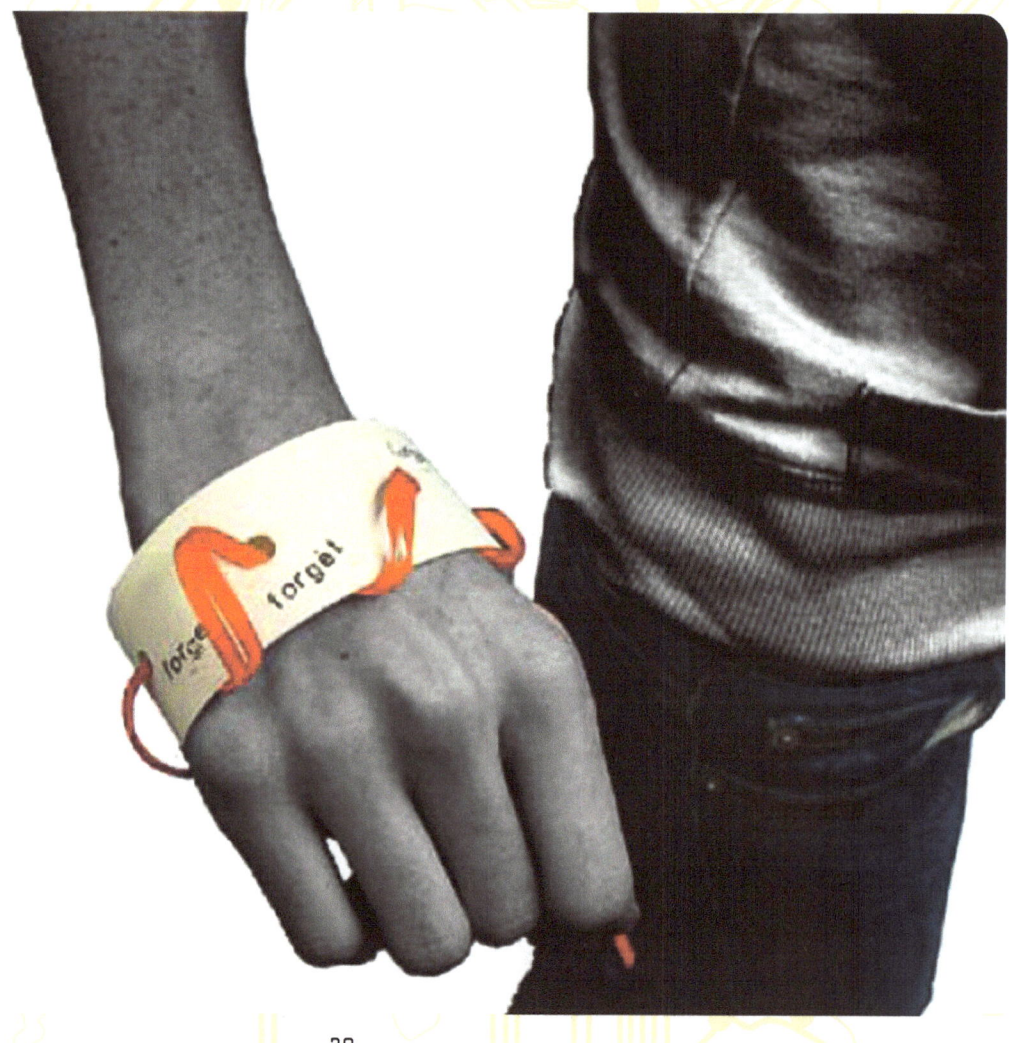

Remember to Forget?
Aoife Ludlow, 2006.

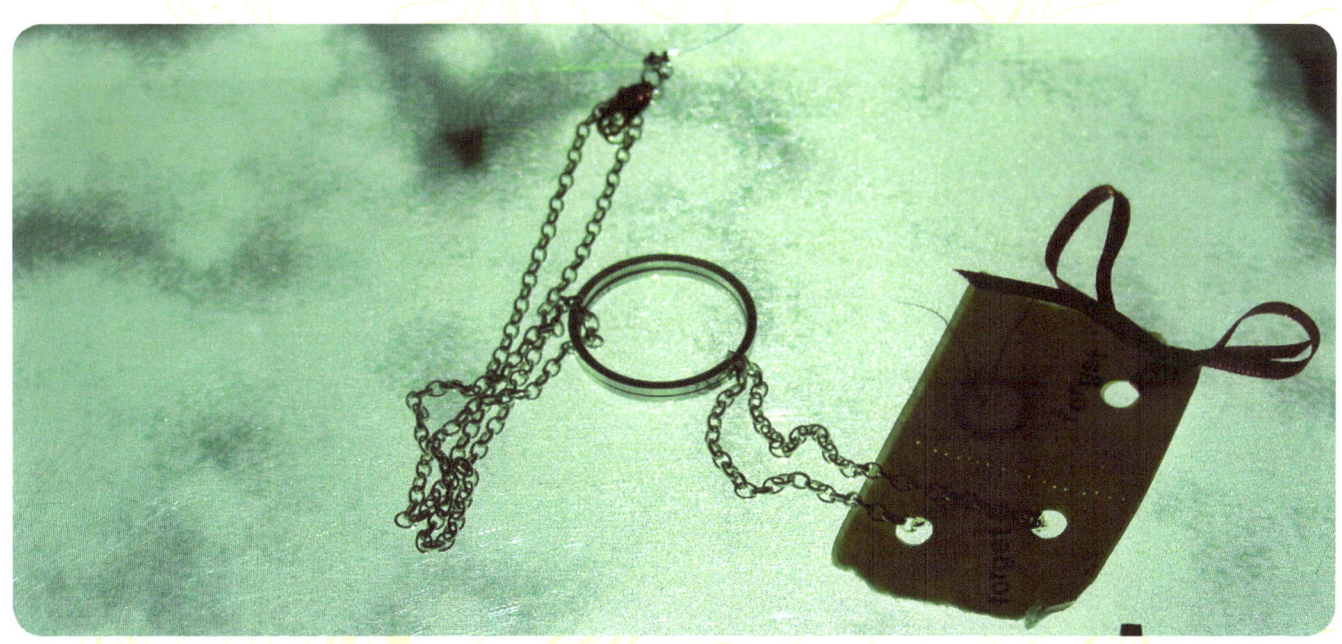

Remember to Forget?

Aoife Ludlow, 2006.

Everyday jewellery tends to be stored in the same place each night. This place is where the objects often move from the periphery of attention to the centre. Could this be the time to promote reflection or consideration, when the object moves from body to box, when it moves to the centre?

Remember to Forget? consists of a jewellery box and related pieces of jewellery which explore notions of memory, change and habit. It adds another communicative/reflective layer to the experience of wearing and the traditional interaction between person, object and container.

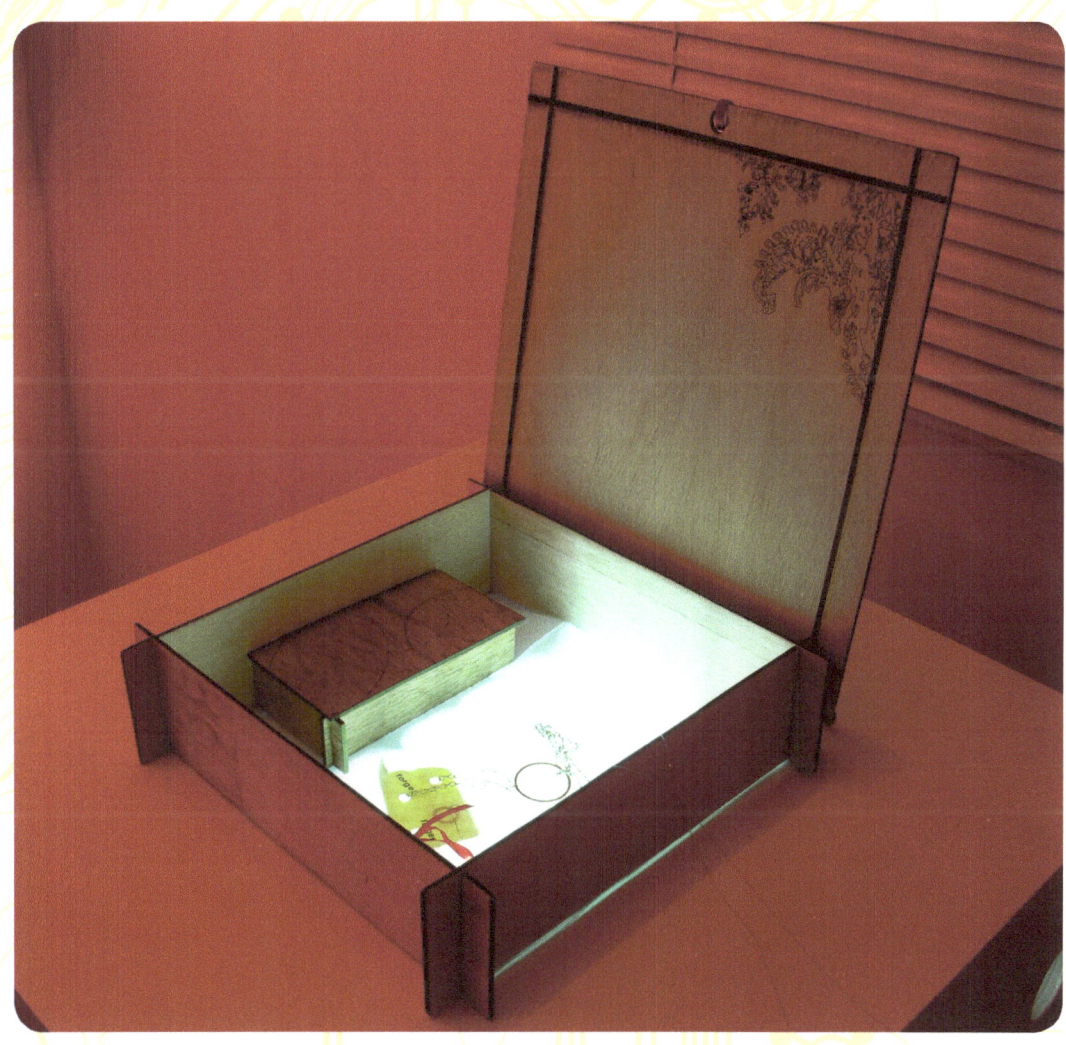

Coded Ornament

Justin Marshall

Through collaboration with Hayles & Howe, a manufacturer of architectural ornamental plasterwork, Marshall has developed a range of plaster mouldings that integrate digital design technologies with traditional manufacturing skills.

The installation Morse, a spiral of dots and dashes, relates to the binary nature of digital information.

A separate work, Penrose Strapping 1, is a stunning contemporary example of traditional strapwork with scrolls, arabesques, and loops.

Justin Marshall's practice spans sculpture, installation and design. His recent work has been ceramic or plaster based. Marshall is currently Research Fellow in 3D digital production at University College, Falmouth.

www.justinmarshall.co.uk
www.autonomatic.org.uk

Penrose Strapping 1

Justin Marshall, 2006.

A Penrose aperiodic tiling system was used as the basis for this plaster strapwork design. This type of tiling allows complex non repeating tessellations to be produced from only two units.

The system also allows an infinite variety of different designs to be produced from these basic units, which gives each consumer the opportunity to develop their own unique strapwork design.

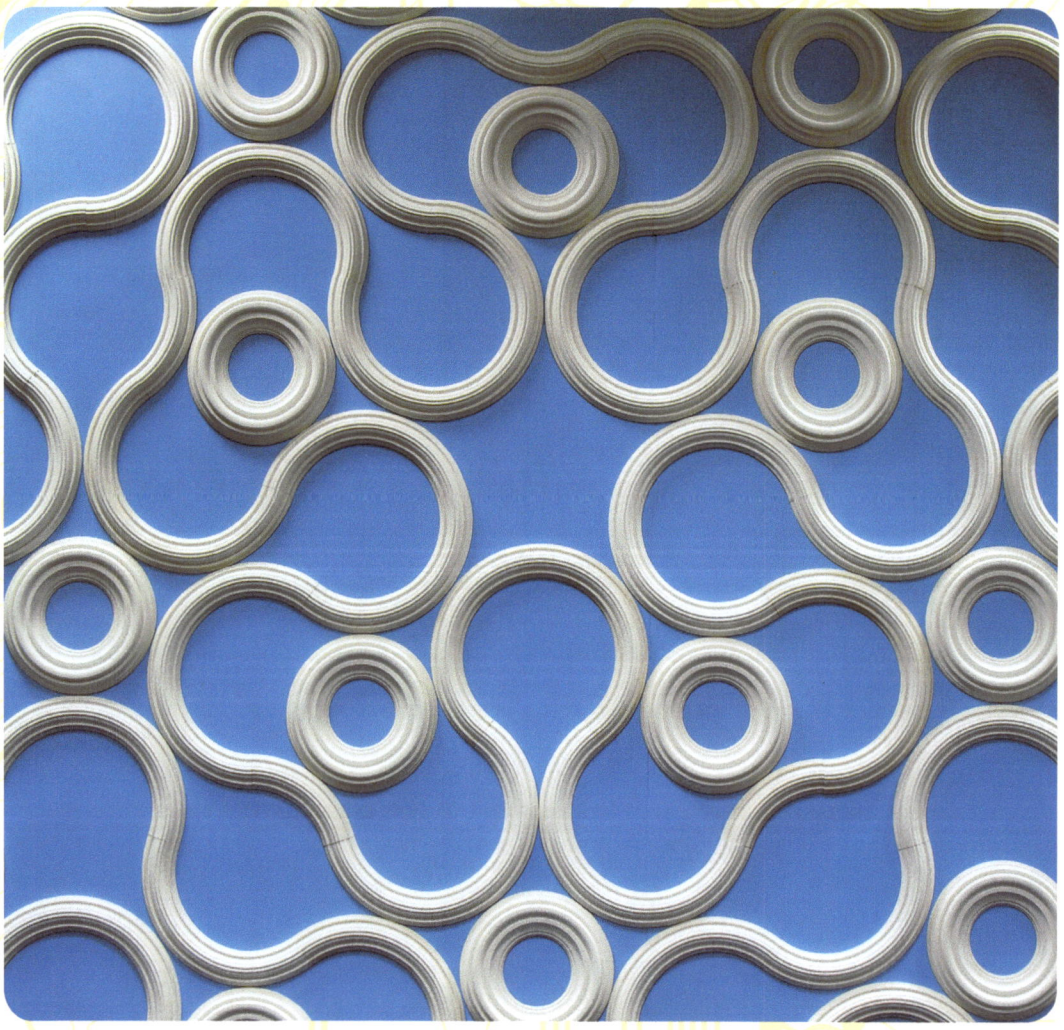

Penrose Strapping 1
Justin Marshall, 2006.

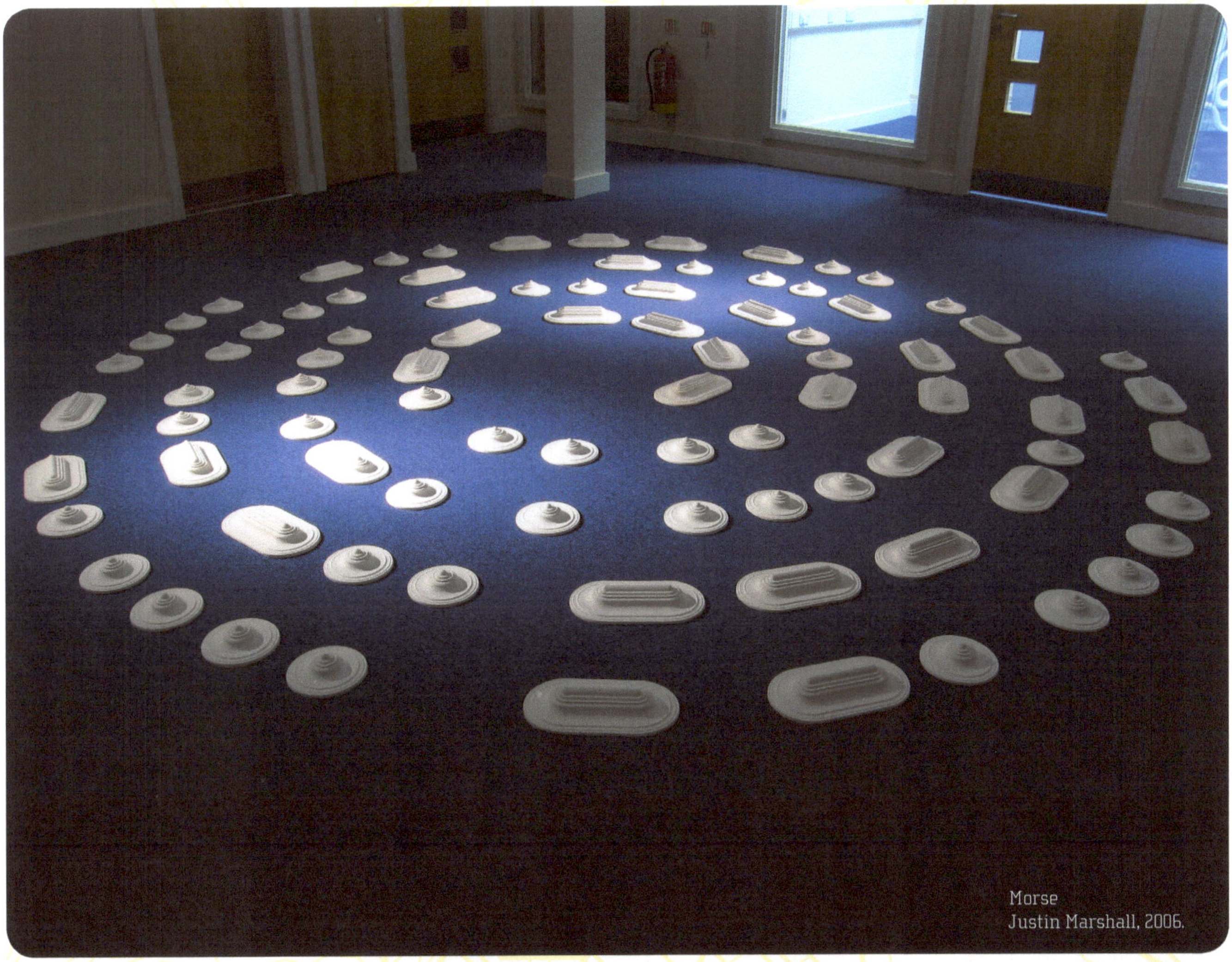

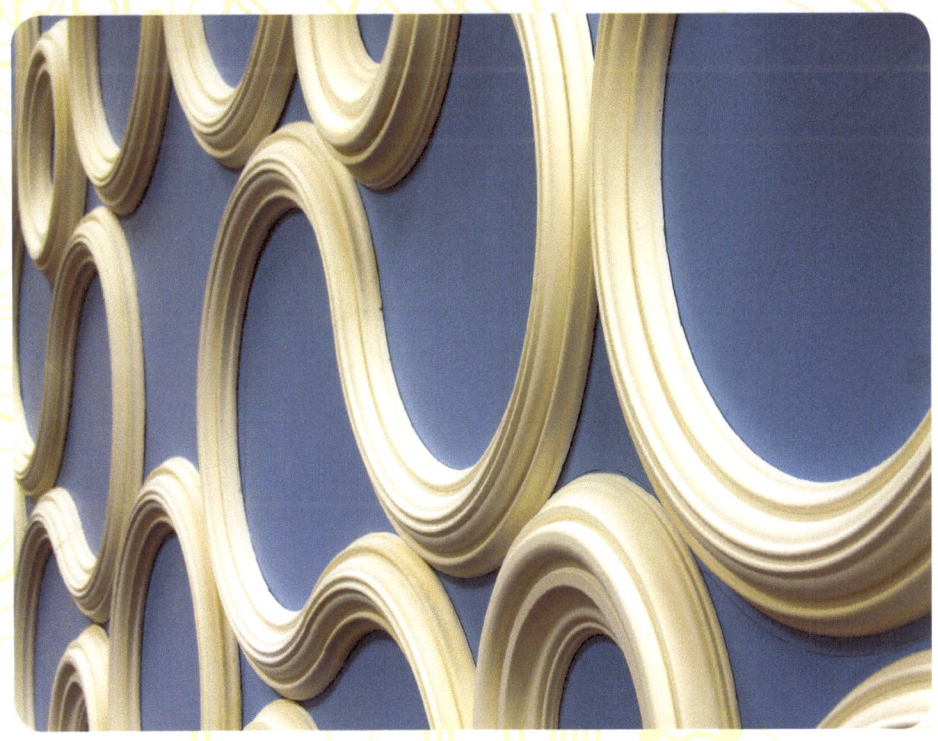

Morse
Justin Marshall, 2006.

'Morse (above)

Justin Marshall, 2006.

Morse' makes reference to the binary nature of digital information. The installation is based on two plaster units: a dot and a dash. These units were developed in CAD and CNC milled.

The message encoded reads "What hath God wrought" which is the text of the first telegraph message ever transmitted. This was sent by Samuel F.B. Morse on May 24, 1844, from Washington, DC, to Baltimore. The message is a biblical quotation from Numbers 23:23.

Penrose Strapping 1 (right)
Justin Marshall, 2006.

LSD Drive

Simon Blackmore

Blackmore's custom-built LSD Drive is able to interpret lost data on apparently useless CDs, and process it using a program written in the Open Source software, SuperCollider.

Light Sensitive Disk Drive is a fully functioning prototype hardware/software product that explores ideas of technological progress, technological waste and its environmental impact. CDs in various states of degradation can be played on the drive to produce different sounds from the lost areas of data.

Blackmore is based in Manchester. Since 2001, he has been reinventing the function or image of culturally iconic objects to make sculptures, including converting a caravan into a gallery, making audio laptops from logs and turning a pole lathe into a musical instrument.

www.simonblackmore.net

LSD Drive

Simon Blackmore, 2006.

A CD drive taken from an old pc has been taken apart. The complex motors have been made to function again using hand coded microcontrollers. The laser that normally reads the data of the CD has been replaced by a light sensor that detects changes in light levels through the disk.

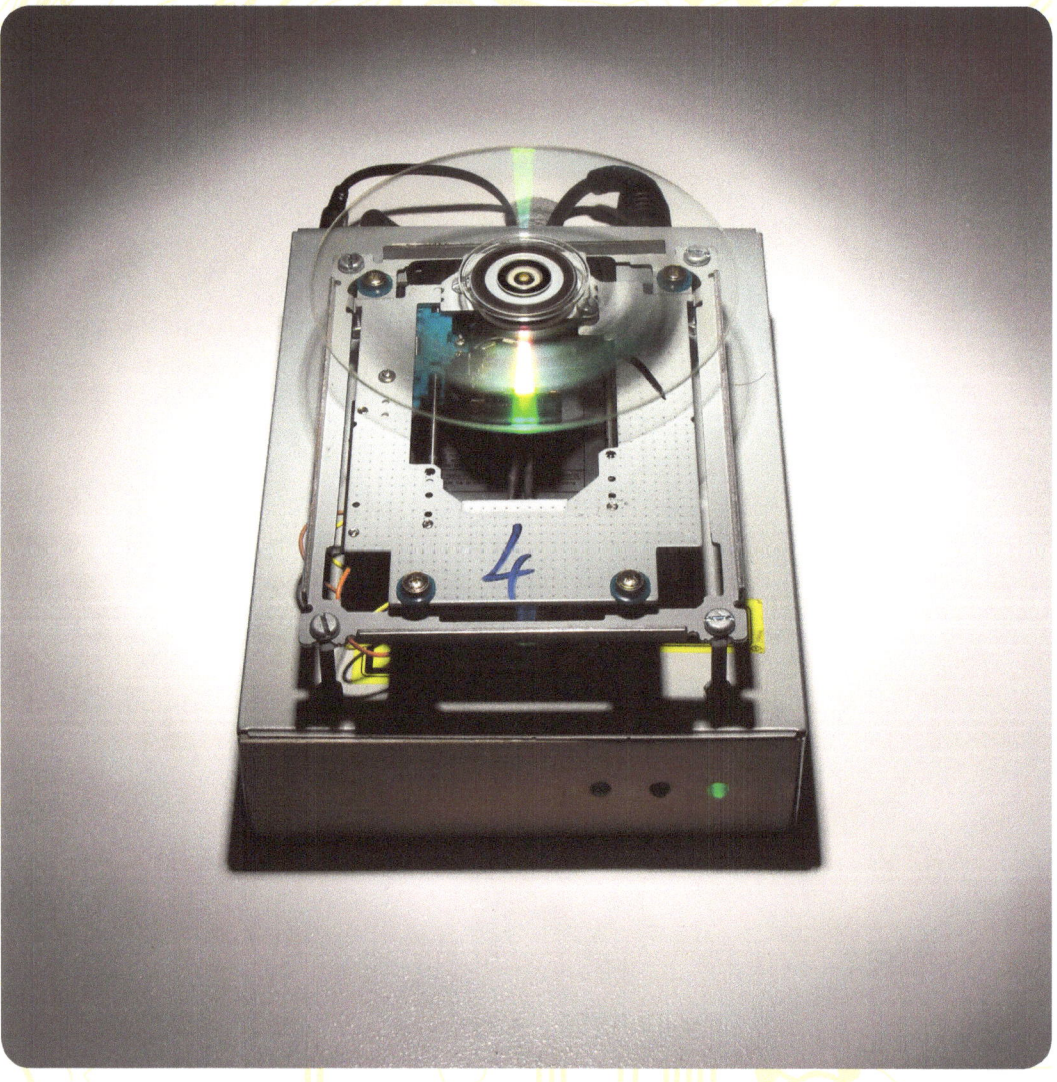

LSD Drive
Simon Blackmore, 2006.

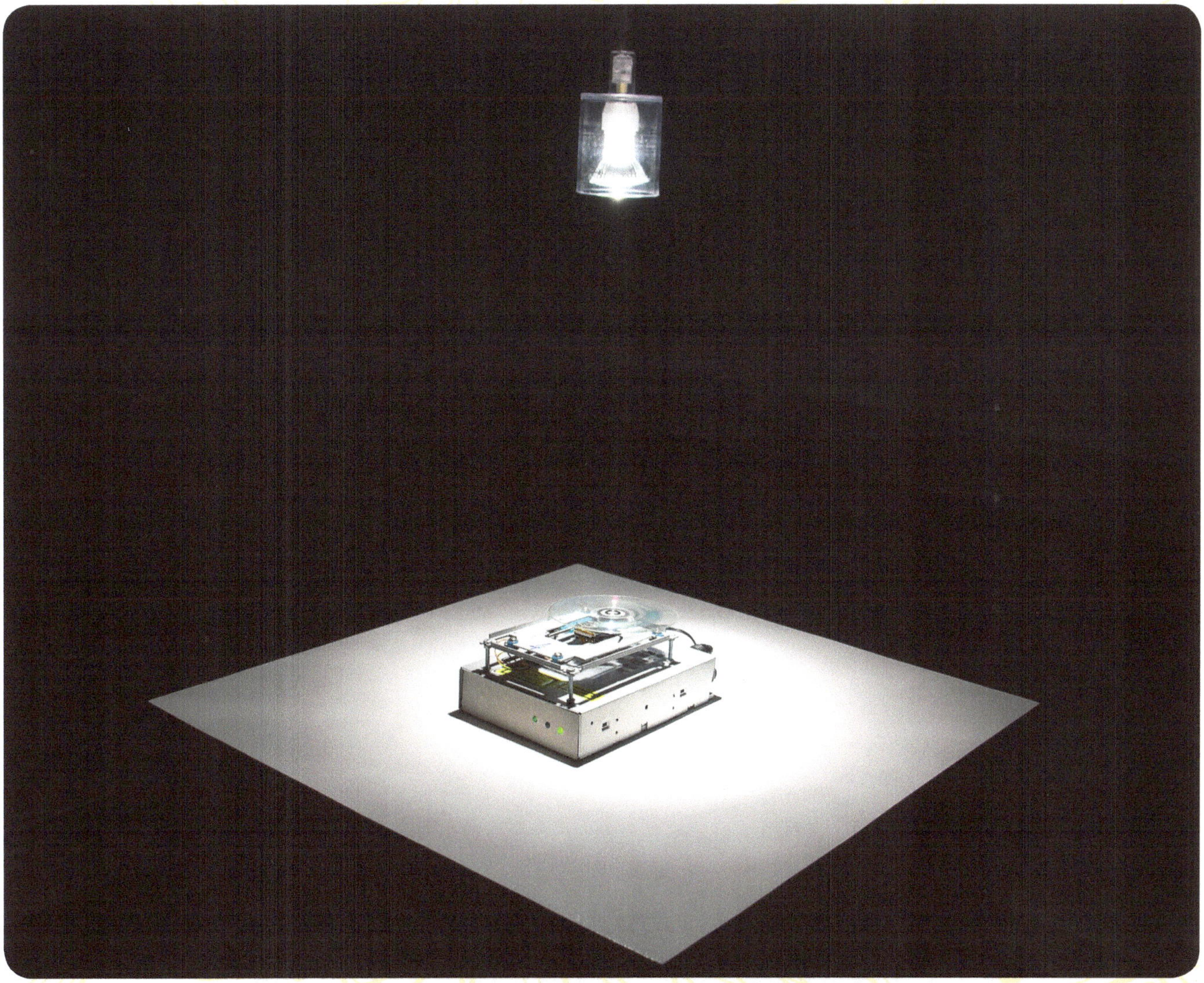

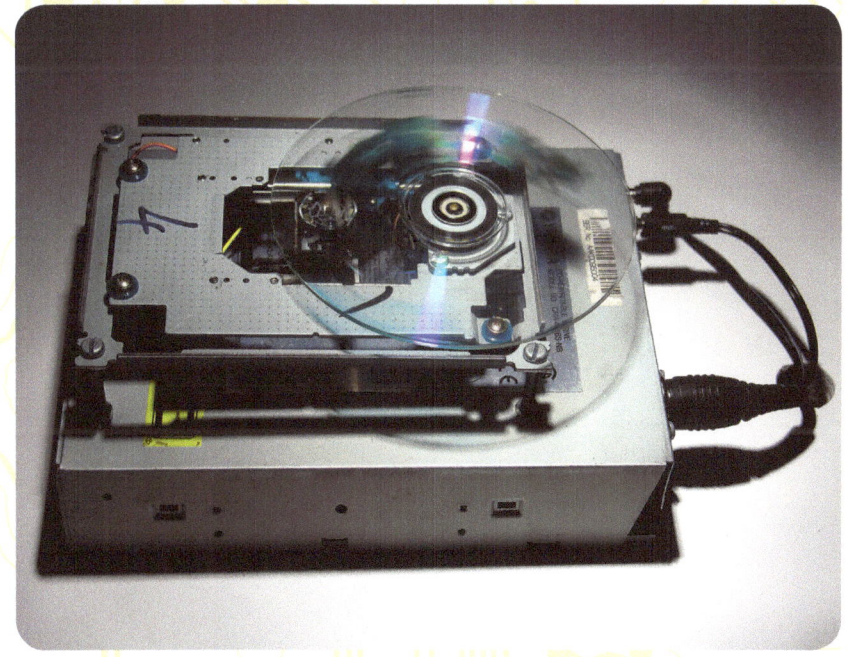

LSD Drive

Simon Blackmore, 2006.

By detecting the amount of light that falls through the disk, the drive is able to read the areas of lost data on a disk. This information is sent to a computer as midi data and then processed by a custom program written in the Open Source software application, 'SuperCollider'. This information is used to sequence the playback and mixing of live recordings of the space the work is exhibited in.

Ibuki – Presence in a Sigh

Masaru Tabei and Yasuno Miyauchi

This is a sound object that you don't hear with your ears but by vibrations transmitted through the body. The material used and the shape of the object invite the visitor to embrace it and to rest their chin on it. Vibrations are transmitted through the jaw and the sound can be heard. The experience generates an overwhelming sense of the small object's huge presence.

Masaru Tabei was born in 1978 in Gumma, Japan and is currently studying an M.A. in Interactive Media at IAMAS (Institute of Advanced Media Art and Science), Japan. Yasuno Miyauchi was born in 1980 in Tokyo, Japan and is currently studying time-based media at IAMAS and also studied Music Composition at Tokyo Gakugei University. Ibuki – Presence in a Sigh has previously been shown in the exhibition 'Source of Life' at IAMAS, Yokohama in 2006.

www.hyougensya.com

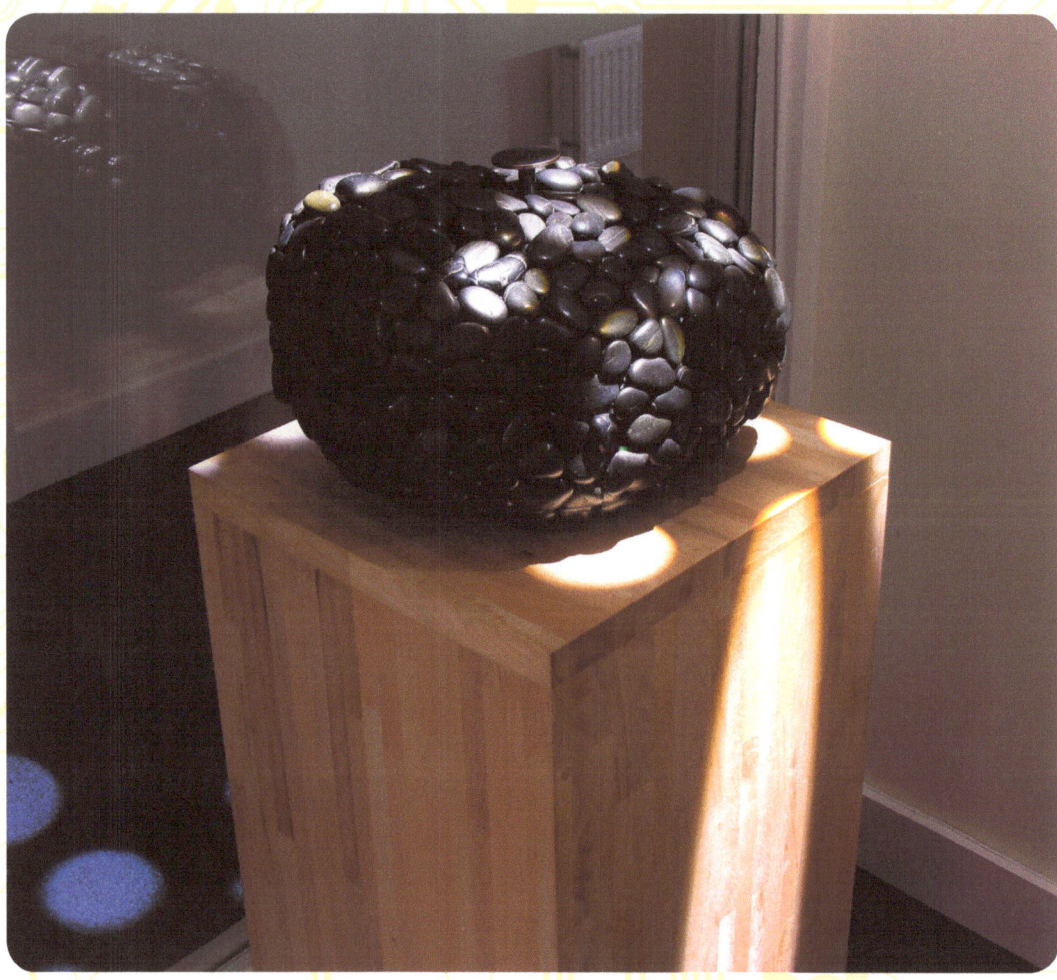

Ibuki – Presence in a Sigh
Masaru Tabei and Yasuno
Miyauchi, 2006.

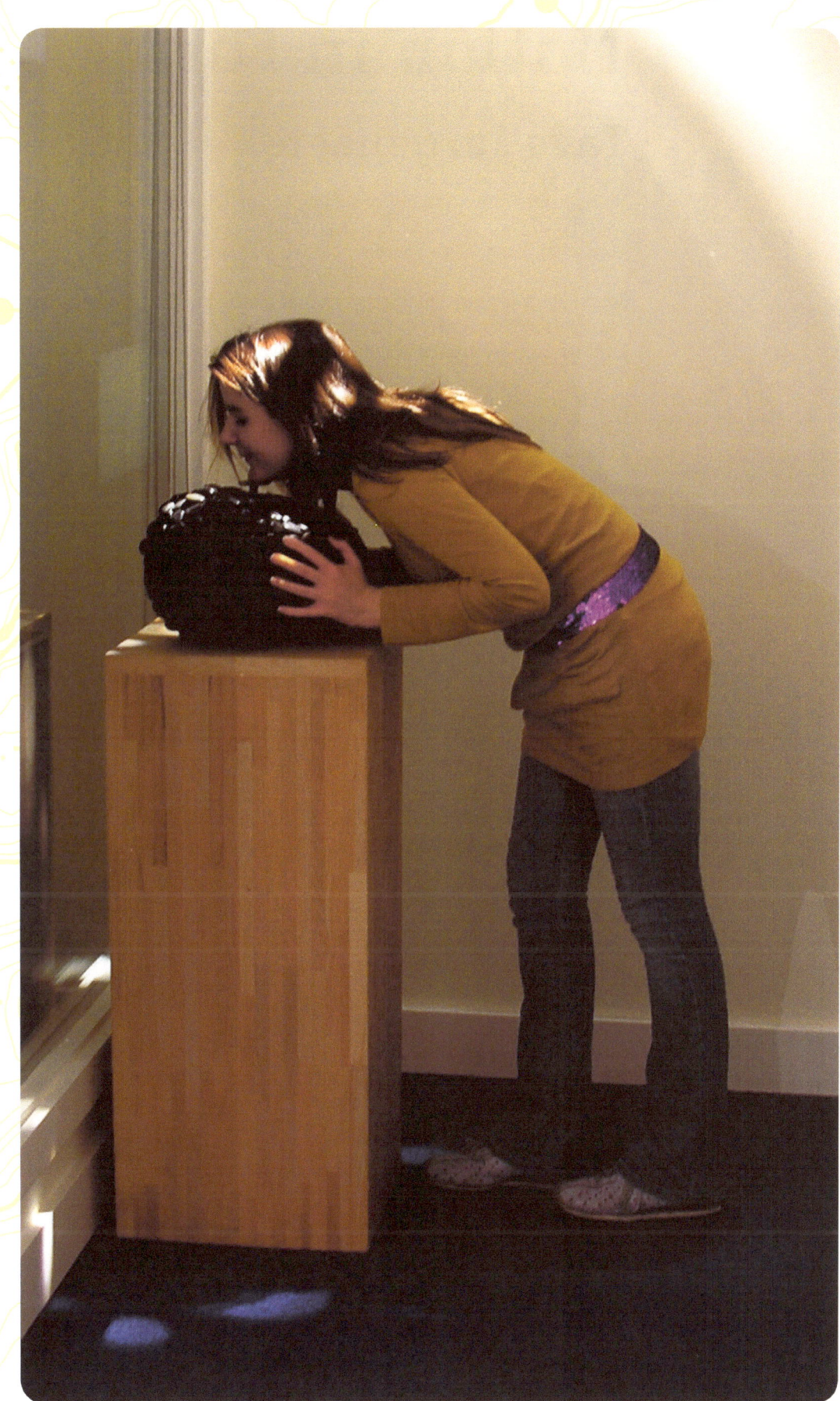

Ibuki – Presence in a Sigh

Masaru Tabei and Yasuno Miyauchi, 2006.

Bone conduction is the transmission of sound to the inner ear through the bones of the skull. Some hearing aids employ bone conduction, achieving an effect equivalent to hearing directly by means of the ears. Recently, companies have embraced bone conduction for consumer products. A cell phone handset is on sale in Japan that lets users listen by pressing it against their jaws.

In this work the artists' strive for a new way of listening. They want the user to realize the presence of his/her own body, and understand that the whole body resonates with the sounds of the world.

Motion in Form

Tavs Jørgensen

Using a data glove and micro scriber the artist has made three dimensional drawings that describe objects in space. The results have been output using CNC (Computer Numerical Control) milling, before being moulded and realised in materials such as glass or ceramic.

Jørgensen's projects merge traditional methods in furniture making, ceramics and foundry work with new technologies such as Rapid Prototyping, Digitising and Motion Capture. The aesthetics of his work reflect the construction process used to make them.

Jørgensen is currently Research Fellow in 3D Digital Production at the Autonomatic Research Cluster, University College Falmouth. He was a finalist for the Bombay Sapphire Prize, 2008.

www.oktavius.co.uk

Motion in Form

Tavs Jørgensen, 2006.

The project builds on earlier research using the G2 Microscribe digitizer to make three-dimensional drawings. However, 'motion capture' extends the possibilities as it enables unrestricted movement and adds the facility of tracking the curves from all ten digits, which provides far more expressive and dynamic results.

These paths are fed directly into a CAD program to be used as basic 'frames' for constructing skins or solid forms. The emphasis of this work is on the 'complete' making process, using the digital tools in synergy with the material knowledge of traditional creative practices.

Another approach of this project was to record everyday motions with the hands. The action of taking a mug from the draining board and using a tea towel to wipe it was captured. This data was then digitally printed onto tea towels (in background, right).

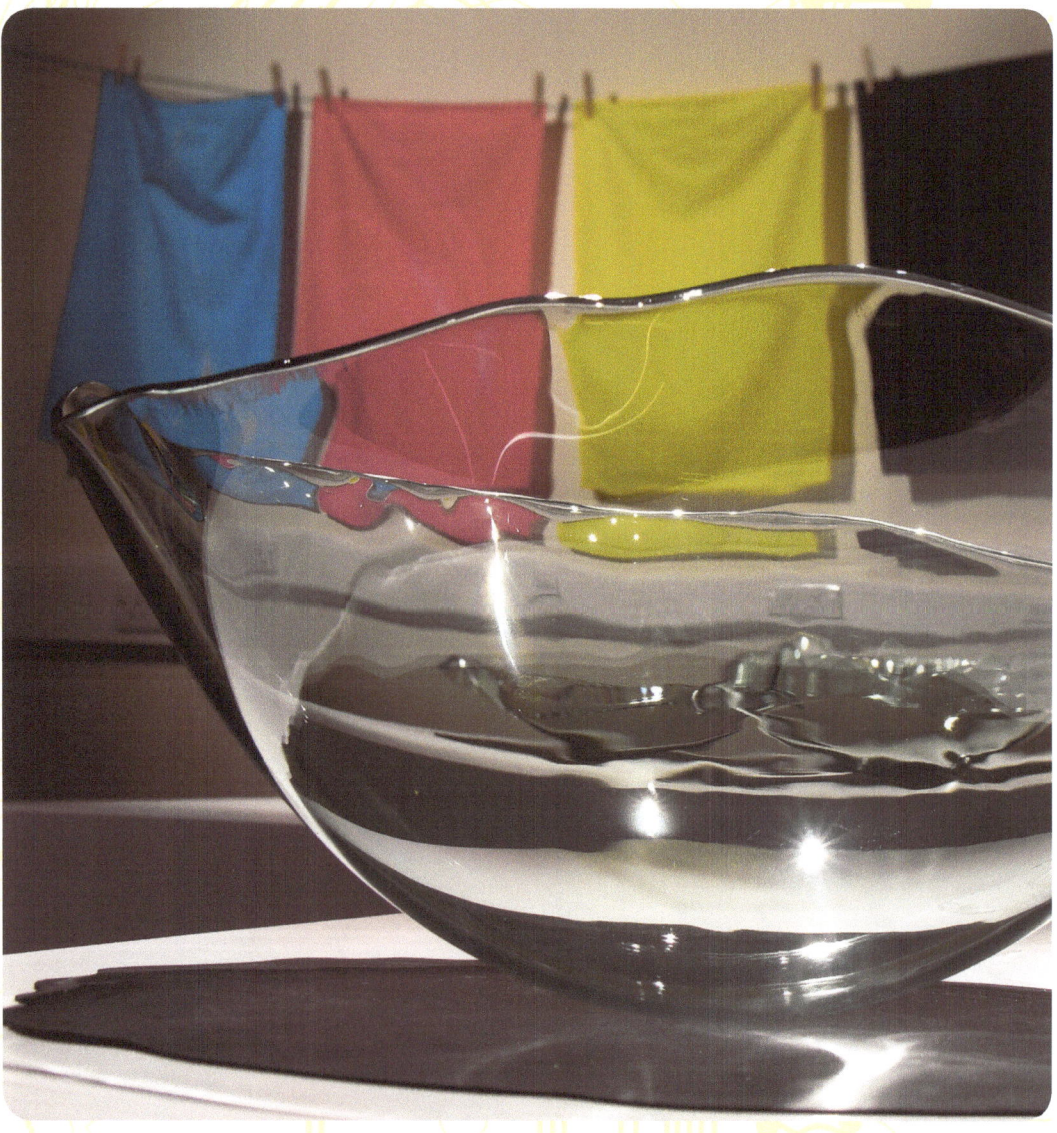

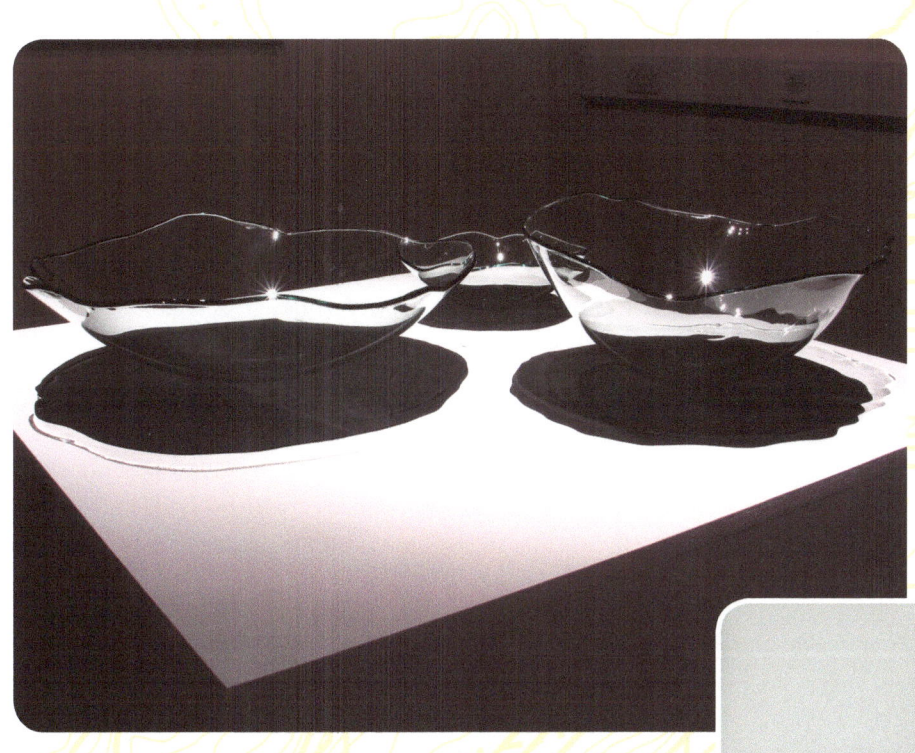

Motion in Form

Tavs Jørgensen, 2006.

A line is drawn in space. This is extruded in CAD to define a surface. This is unfolded and laser cut from very thin stainless steel to form a collar - a physical representation of the 3D line. This is set it in plaster and a disk of glass set onto it. As the glass is heated in a kiln it goes soft and gravity causes it to gently flow down and sit exactly on the rim of the collar. This results in a bowl form (above) that represents the digital recording but also makes use of the physical nature of the glass.

A set of stools (right) where the seating surfaces have been milled from the data captured using the ShapeHand™ system (middle, right).

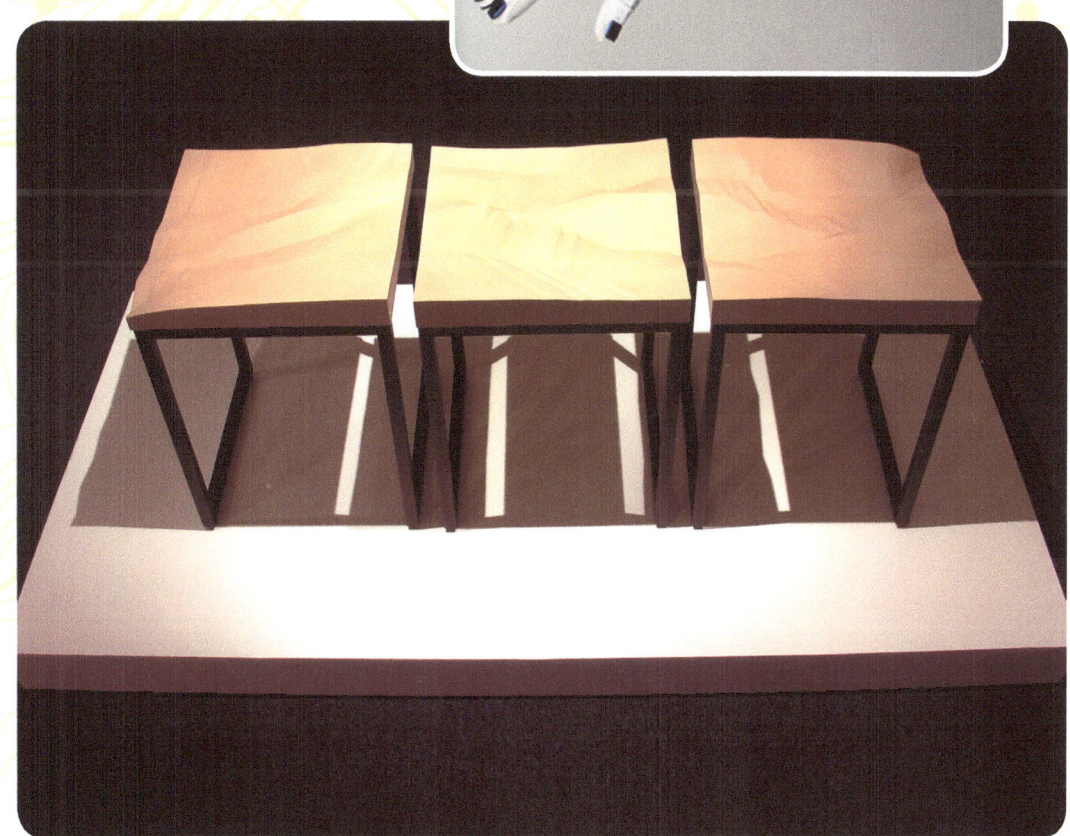

Sheep Jet Head

Brit Bunkley

Sheep Jet Head is a computer generated map of a passing jet plane flying across a sheep's head and body as it stands in a rural landscape. By capturing invented scenes in a believable but slightly skewed setting, Bunkley illustrates his view of globalised modern life.

Bunkley is Head of Sculpture and a lecturer in digital media at the Quay School of the Arts, UCOL in Wanganui, New Zealand. He began using computers as a design tool for public sculpture in 1992. His work uses various 3D rapid prototype printing technologies, traditional castings and CNC (Computer Numerical Control) milling.

www.britbunkley.com

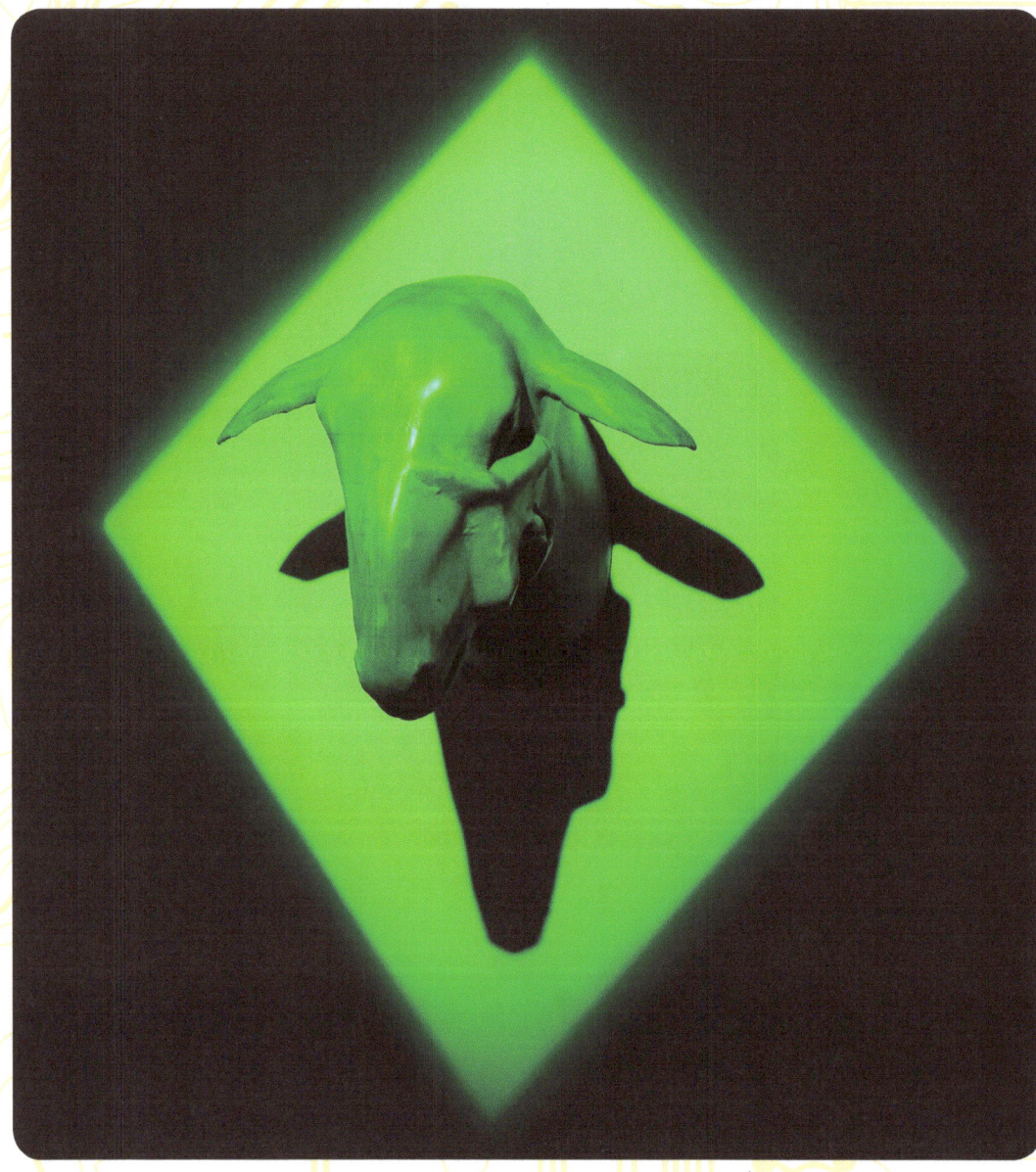

Sheep Jet Head

Brit Bunkley, 2006.

Sheep Jet Head is a series of interrelated artworks created with 3D software that incorporates a displacement map of a jet plane on a 3D model of a sheep within a rural landscape. In these works, the same 3D file is output in different media - in this case as a physical object and as a projected animation.

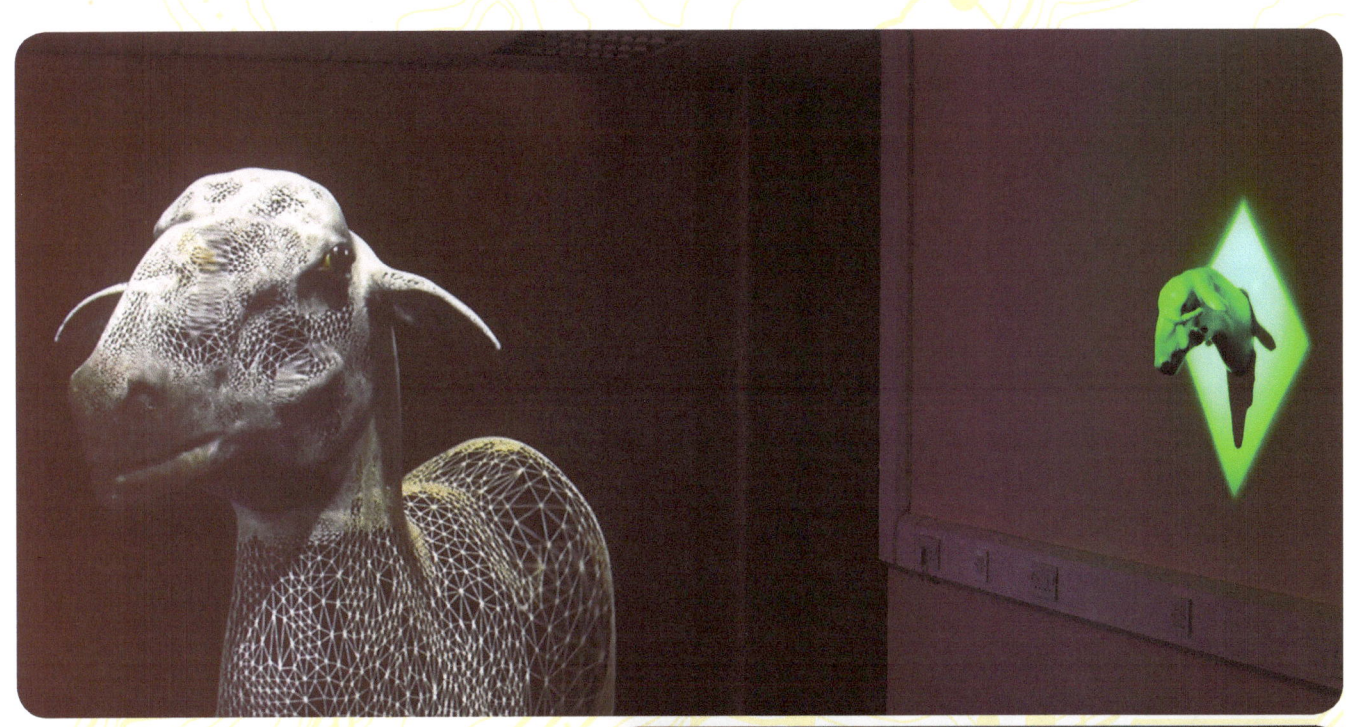

Sheep Jet Head

Brit Bunkley, 2006.

The physical object was fabricated by Laminated Object Manufacturing (LOM). This is a manufacturing process that uses a laser to cut successive cross-sections of an object from layers of paper applied from a roller with an adhesive coating on the backside. The laser cuts the outline of the cross-sections that form the object. Once the laser is done cutting the object, it then proceeds to create hatch marks, or cubes that surround the object. Once the object has been cut, the next step involves decubing. When all of the cubes have been removed, the part is sanded down and a lacquer is used to seal the part. The finished part has a surface and density similar to wood.

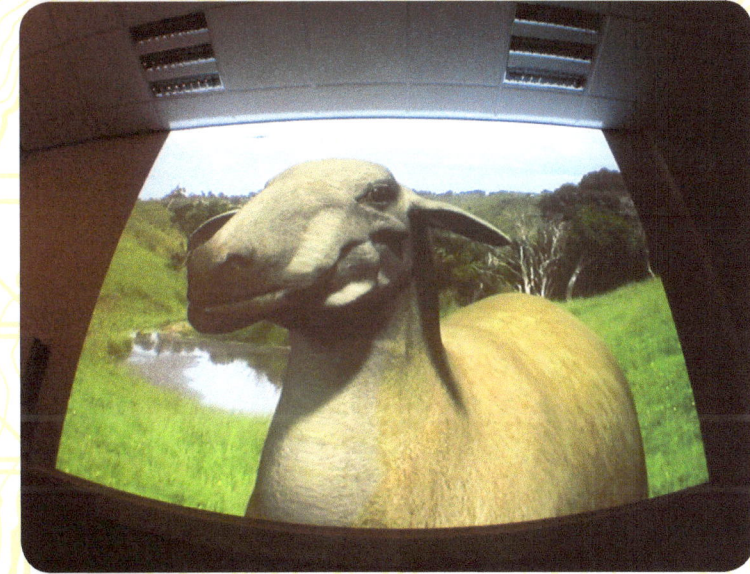

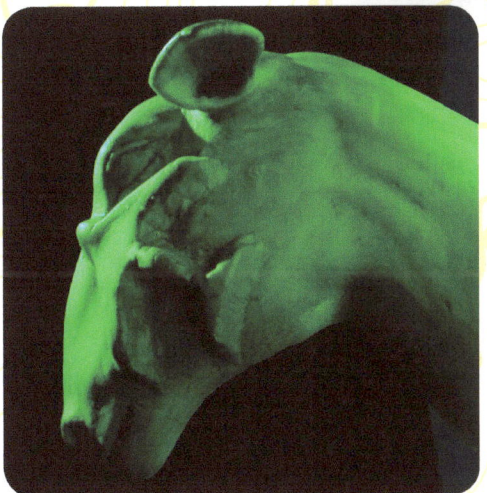

Holy Ghost

FutureFactories

Lionel T. Dean continues the FutureFactories theme of organic growth with a design that's in a constant state of evolution. In Holy Ghost, the back and arms of an iconic chair design have been morphed to create a very different view of an everyday object and a new object of desire. Dean has frozen the real time generation of these new forms to create two 'hard copies' of the design using Rapid Prototyping technology.

Dean is Designer in Residence at Huddersfield University. Future Factories is a digital manufacturing concept for the mass individualisation of products. Future Factories has had exhibitions in London and Milan. Previously Dean worked as an automotive designer for Pininfarina in Italy, before launching his own consultancy business.

www.futurefactories.com

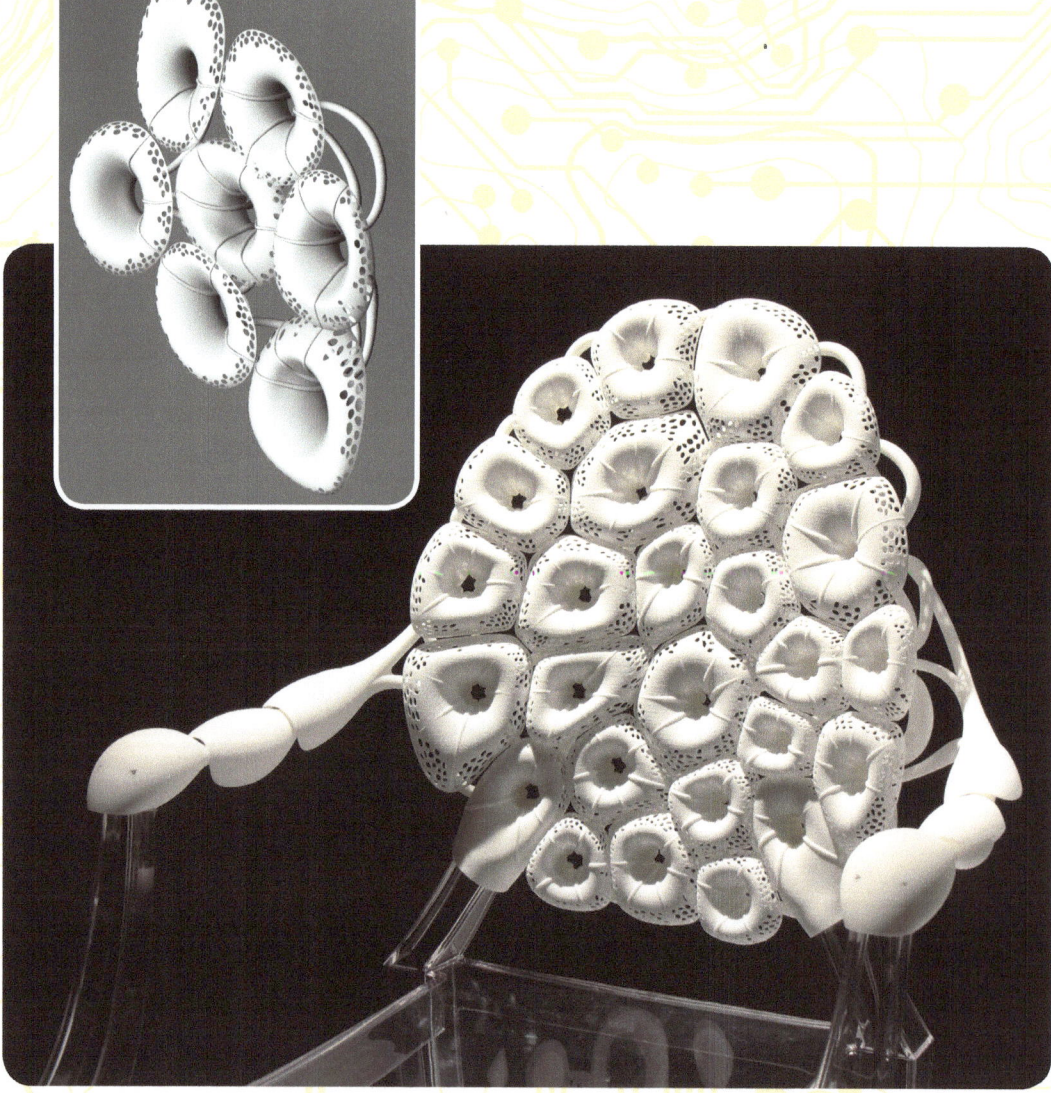

Holy Ghost (rendering)
FutureFactories, 2006.

Holy Ghost
FutureFactories, 2006.

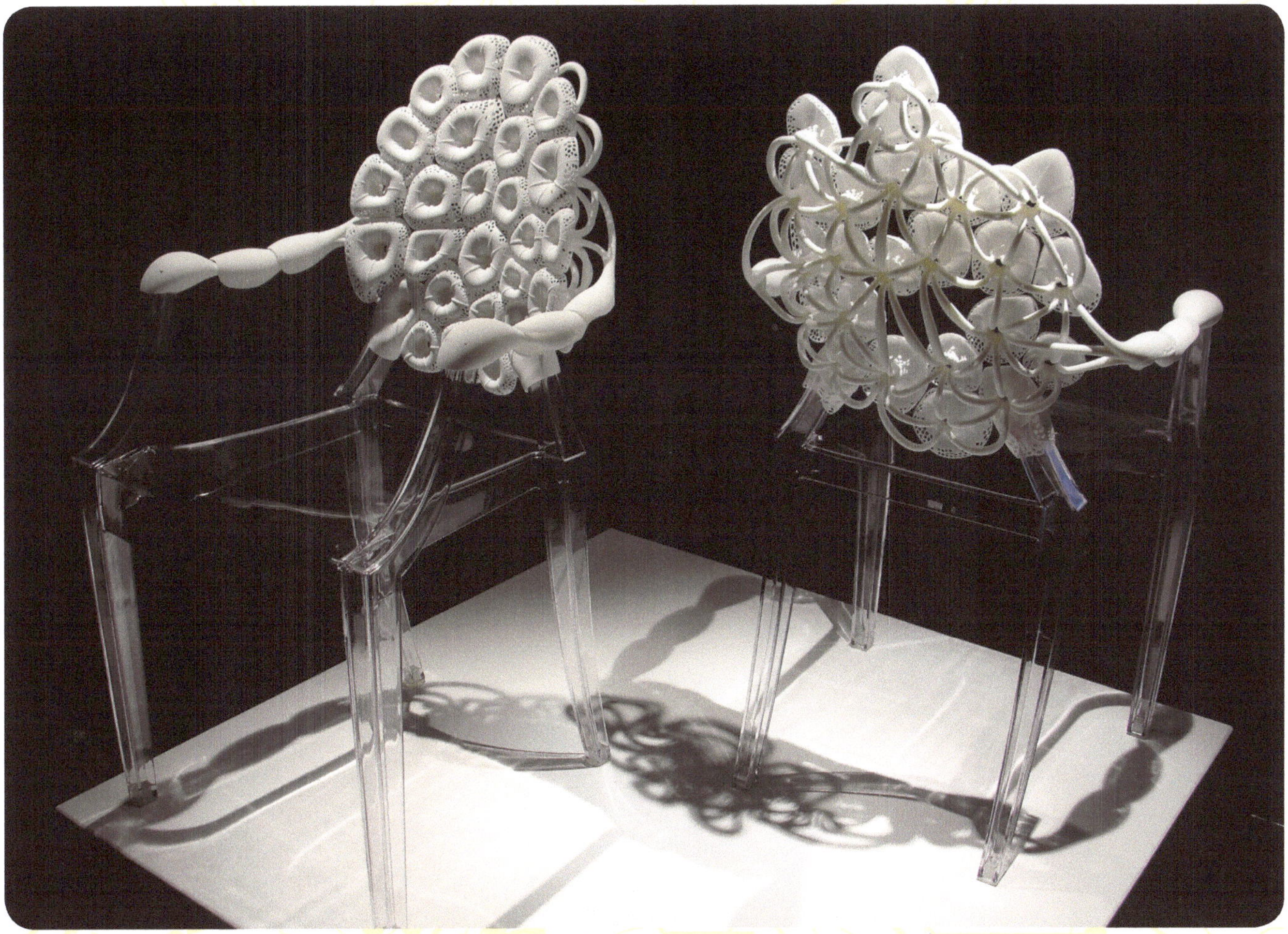

Holy Ghost

FutureFactories, 2006.

This project mutates the Louis Ghost chair (designed by Philippe Starck and produced by Kartell). As its name suggests, the chair is in the Louis XVI style in accordance with Dean's recent work in the 'nouveau baroque' style. This work plays with notions of metamorphosis, symbiosis and parasitism. The modified chairs create a new reading of both an everyday object and an iconic object of desire.

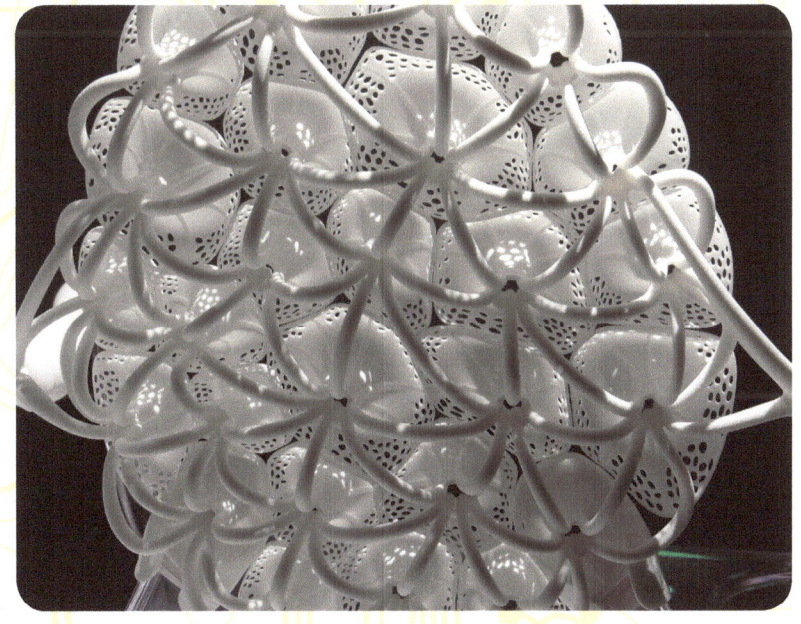

.MGX by Materialise

Assa Ashuach, Arik Levy, Naomi Kaempfer & Dan Yeffet

Materialise are specialists in the field of Rapid Prototyping. But with their .MGX brand they have been making major waves in the design world with computer-manufactured designs for lighting and decorative objects.

Knowledge of digital tools has allowed these designers to shape and calculate complex, functional structures. The rapid manufacturing techniques of Materialise have enabled these extraordinary shapes to be turned into reality, and have unleashed a new era of mass-customised, design-to-order products.

www.materialise-mgx.com

Black_Honey.MGX

Arik Levy graduated with distinction in industrial design from Art Center Europe in Switzerland. Arik works both as a scientist and a poet. Innovation, simplicity and experimentation permit him to create the new and translate the concepts into experience both in the art and the design world

www.ldesign.fr

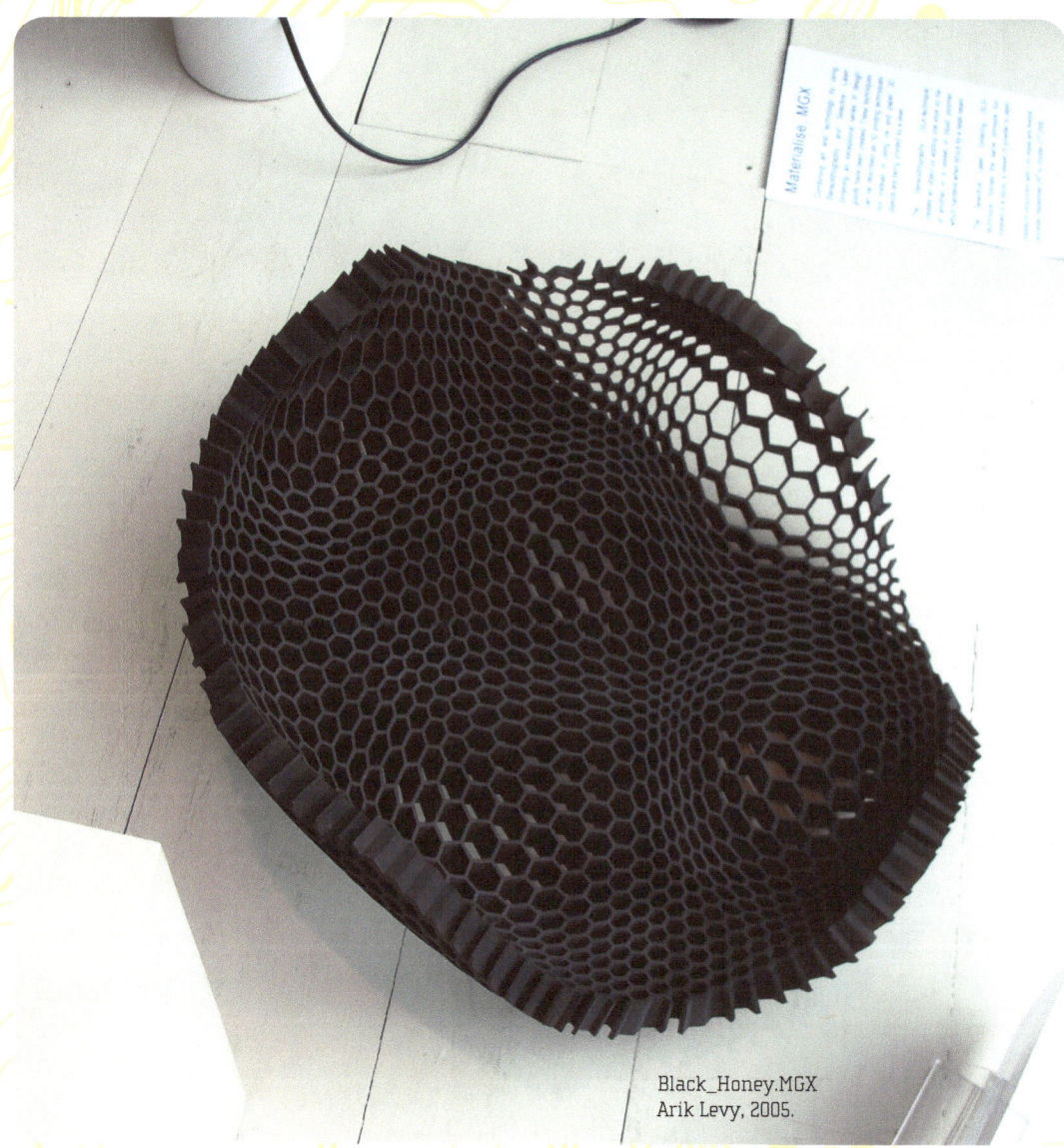

Black_Honey.MGX
Arik Levy, 2005.

Ratio.MGX (top, lit)

Naomi Kaempfer studied industrial design at The Hadassah technical college, Jerusalem and at the Design Academy in Eindhoven, Netherlands. She now works as Head of and Art Director of Materialise.MGX, Leuven, Belgium.

www.materialise-mgx.com

Palea.MGX (red, bottom) &

Hidden.MGX (inset, right)

Dan Yeffet has studied at the Bezalel Academy of Art and Design, Jerusalem and graduated at The Gerrit Rietveld Academie, Amsterdam. He is director of Jelly Lab Studio, a design studio located in Amsterdam that specialises in product and interior design.

www.jellylab.com

Omi.MGX (middle, unlit)

Assa Ashuach was born in Israel, he studied product design at the Bezalel Academy of Art and Design and at the Royal College of Art and Design. His studio focuses on three main tracks: products for companies, collaboration with architects and self-production.

www.assaashuach.com/

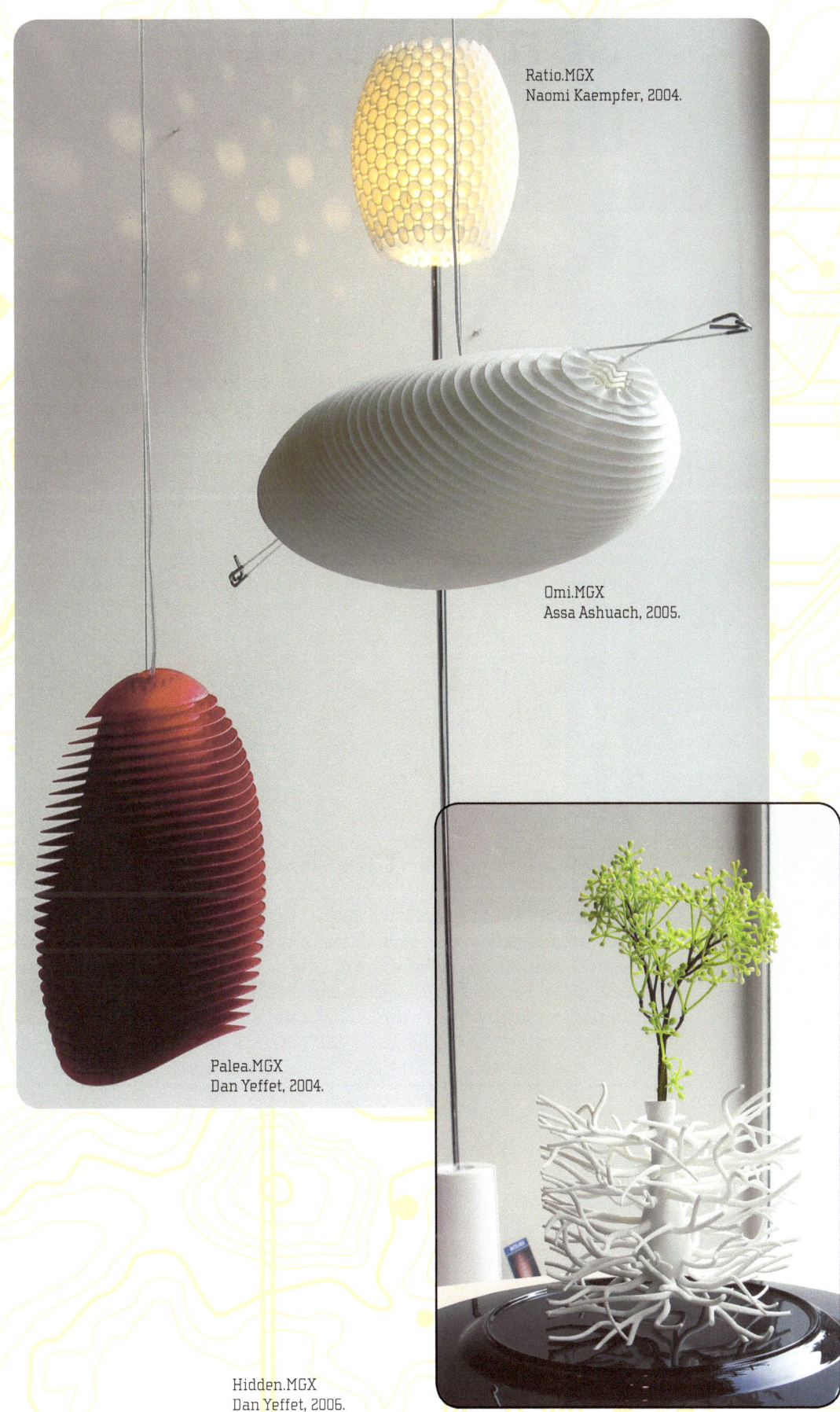

Ratio.MGX
Naomi Kaempfer, 2004.

Omi.MGX
Assa Ashuach, 2005.

Palea.MGX
Dan Yeffet, 2004.

Hidden.MGX
Dan Yeffet, 2006.

Contributing Organisations

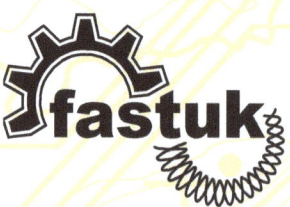

Fast-uk is an artist-led organisation dedicated to promoting and encouraging artists that use digital and or electronic technologies in some part of their practice. Founded in 1997, originally to support sculptors working with 3D computer technologies, Fast-uk has evolved to support the creative application of technology to practices stemming from or working between the boundaries of sculpture, architecture and industrial design. Based in Manchester, Fast-uk aims to work throughout the Northwest by forming important partnerships with artists, educational institutions and other organisations. Fast-uk supports those working in this area through exhibition, networking and professional development opportunities and through disseminating publications and critical discourse.

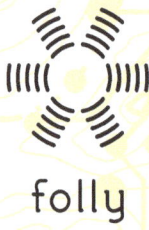

folly

folly is a leading digital arts organisation. Working in the North West of England and online, folly is committed to enabling new audiences to explore art through technology. As specialists in the creative use of technology and arts participation online, folly's programme showcases excellence in web-based work, still and moving digital image, sound, animation and a range of new and emerging media such as GPS, RFID, moblogging and more. Focused on Cumbria, Lancashire & online, communicating with and working in partnership with a regional, national and international audience, they develop and deliver content not only online but through an ambitious distributed programme of workshops, events, exhibitions, research and consultancy work.

Credits and Acknowledgments

Perimeters, Boundaries and Borders was made possible through funding and support from Arts Council England NW, MIRIAD, Lancaster City Council, and was hosted at CityLab.

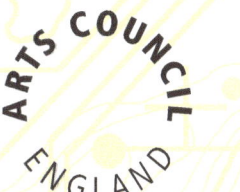 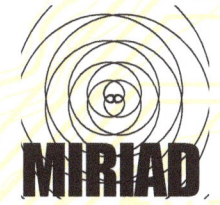 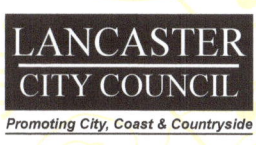

Perimeters, Boundaries and Borders was presented in partnership with folly as part of the f.city festival of digital culture.

F.CITY

FESTIVAL OF DIGITAL CULTURE

Photo Credits

Unless otherwise identified all photographs and graphic images are the work of John Marshall.

p. 24 (top and bottom) photography Simon Husslein
p. 28 (top) renderings by NIO Architecten
p. 30 photography by Aoife Ludlow
p. 39 (middle) photography Tavs Jørgensen
p. 41 (middle and bottom) photography Simon Husslein
p. 42 (top) rendering by Lionel T. Dean

Thanks

This project would not have been possible without the help and contribution of a number of people. We would like to thank each of the individual practitioners who participated in the exhibition. Fast-uk would also like to thank the team at folly for their work to make the exhibition a success. Additional thanks go to John Hyatt for his opening remarks at the symposium and his continued support for both Fast-uk and folly and to Paul Rodgers whose keynote at the symposium helped frame the critical debates taking place at the intersection of art, design and new technology.

www.ingramcontent.com/pod-product-compliance
Lightning Source LLC
Chambersburg PA
CBHW051102180526
45172CB00002B/736